Robert
GREACEN
Selected & New Poems

Edited by JACK W. WEAVER
Emeritus Professor of English
Winthrop University, South Carolina

Assistant Editor:
REBECCA WEAVER-HIGHTOWER
Assistant Professor of English
University of North Dakota

salmonpoetry

Published in 2006 by
Salmon Poetry,
Cliffs of Moher, County Clare, Ireland
Website: www.salmonpoetry.com
email: info@salmonpoetry.com

ISBN 1 903392 53 5

Cover artwork: Portrait Bust of Robert Greacen 1987 by Robin Buick.
Photography: Robin Buick
Copy text edited by Barbara Brown
Cover Design & Typesetting by Siobhán Hutson

CONTENTS

from A GARLAND FOR CAPTAIN FOX (1975)

from YOUNG MR. GIBBON (1979)

from A BRIGHT MASK: NEW & SELECTED POEMS (1985)

from CARNIVAL AT THE RIVER (1990)

FOREWORD

In 'Finding a Cat', Robert Greacen describes the difficulty of writing a poem as catching a black cat in a dark room and, despite scratches, bringing it out whole. In this metaphor, he was describing the mystery of being a poet, as well as the act of composition. Since Greacen has been as successful in writing critical prose as in creating finely chiselled poems, we can know the works and the taste of the man much better than we can know the man who produced the works. In his launch of *Lunch at the Ivy*, Seamus Heaney focused upon Greacen's three countries of residence: Northern Ireland, Eire, and England and suggested an equivalent persona for each. Heaney's suggestion helps us toward an understanding, but like the cat in the dark room we must scratch a bit more to find it.

Of Scots and Irish stock, Greacen was born in Derry/Londonderry on 24 October 1920 but found himself shuttled back and forth principally between urban Belfast and rural Monaghan. Experiences in city and country furnished materials for later poems and reviews. So did his contacts at Methodist College in Belfast, where he discovered his gift for writing and an interest in leftist politics, and Trinity College in Dublin, where he pursued a practical diploma in Social Studies but contributed to *The Bell* and developed still more friends in artistic circles. Along the way, he loved and was rejected by the Ulster woman whom he designates as 'Irene'. At Trinity, he met and married Patricia Hutchins, a member of the Anglo-Irish ascendancy from County Cork and a future writer of works about James Joyce and Ezra Pound.

Though their marriage was happy in the beginning and produced a daughter, their personal and cultural differences contributed to the inevitable break-up. For Robert, this was followed by a period of depression and some seventeen years in which he published nothing but prose. In a personal essay, he tells of extended counselling and even treatment by means of the hallucinogenic drug LSD. He recovered beautifully and resumed the writing career, which continues to the present day. The final six poems in this volume, in fact, were mailed to the anthology's compiler in June 2004. They make a nice conclusion to the volume, but we can hope the career will continue.

It has been an outstanding compositional career, with individual poems published in Ireland, England, Scotland, France, and the United States, and many volumes in Ireland. As he retired from a career of teaching English as a Foreign Language in London, he was nominated for membership in Aosdána. Now resident in Dublin, he was honoured by his peers on his seventieth birthday (1990) with a commemorative volume of poems. Edited by Rory Brennan, it included works by Seamus Heaney, Stephen Spender, John F. Deane, John Montague, Ulick O'Connor, Michael Longley, Anthony Cronin, Frank Ormsby, Dennis O'Driscoll and Aidan Murphy, among others. In 1995, he was awarded *The Irish Times* Poetry Prize for his *Collected Poems*. He continues to be both productive and honoured for his achievements.

This volume of *Selected & New Poems* uses the *Collected Poems* as basic copy text, at Greacen's request. That volume has poems from *One Recent Evening* (1944), *The Undying Day* (1948), *A Garland for Captain Fox* (1975), *Young Mr. Gibbon* (1979), *A Bright Mask: New & Selected Poems* (1985), and *Carnival at the River* (1990), as well as a group, which are simply identified as *New & Uncollected Poems* (c. 1995). For this volume, I have added selections from *Protestant Without a Horse* (1997), *Captain Fox: A Life* (2000), *Lunch at the Ivy* (2002), and *Shelley Plain* (2003), plus the six manuscript poems of June 2004. Arrangement of the *Selected & New Poems* follows the chronological order of *Collected Poems*, at the suggestion of Dennis O'Driscoll and the request of Greacen. I have included poems which represent the several personae the poet uses – the schoolboy from the province of Ulster, the lyrical poet of personal experience, the biographer of the experiences of others, and the inventor of Captain Fox and his son 'Comrade Ted', Fox's friend Kinsky, and Michael the farmer in County Down. With use of his own lovers, relatives, and friends as poetic subjects, Greacen alternates between an air of detachment and one of involvement. As the reader quickly discovers, the 'air' is merely an authorial stance. Whether speaking in his own voice or through those invented, his view of life emerges, as does that of Yeats and Robert Browning in their monologues. For non-European readers (ignorant Americans, like myself), I have added a few notes to shed light on details, which may mean more to the poet than his readers. I trust that they and the poems in *Selected & New Poems* will help us to find the cat in the dark room, even with a few scratches.

JACK W. WEAVER
Emeritus Professor of English
Winthrop University
Rock Hill, South Carolina
U.S.A.

ONE RECENT EVENING

(1944)

ONE RECENT EVENING

One recent evening, when time and space were standing still,
He crossed the road flanked by air-raid rubble,
And came to a bridge where water stood below.
The sky was flushed with red and very spacious.

The soldiers paced—one of them with bayonet fixed—
Around the firm, broad-breasted, sand-bag fort.
(His brother had defiled the earth.)
The sound of trumpets slashed the dim, horizon lines.

And then he fled the war's impact for individuals—
How it sent one to signal across seas from an oil-tanker,
Another with wound and suitcase from a line of lean houses ...
Tongues of air or sea, of land or fear, divide and conquer us.

Walking beside the river, he forgot the shells that poise
In the city of his alternate love and hate:
He forgot the obscenities of roof and window,
The mad catharsis of the thoroughfares.

Men must not weep, he thought, or show a too great love
For those who sleep under debris or beside ditches ...
'It is feared the death-roll will be heavy'.
Official anguish has no eyes to wipe.

And he, being then an observer, dazed by lack of sleep,
Was conscious only of his unwilling senses,
Of his refusal to accept man's malice or stupidity ...
While the soldiers paced—one of them with bayonet fixed.

THE ALIEN WORLD

O I was tense and loving then
When the whole wild grief of autumn swept
And put again her likeness on the rack of memories.
I was taut with fear that summer evening,
Numb as a plate of glass, dead as a cigarette stub,
As fingering the last letter, I stepped into a vacant future,
Knowing no other future than the sunlight on her hair.
Then, for a long dull moment, time ran cold
While rain swished on the indifferent city,
And the ghosts of war sidled through empty streets.
So now, fearing as then for each new future,
I hear the traffic lurch, the windows shiver,
The hurt dogs whine, the brakes pull short ...
And now, as then, the fast world tense with reeling
Spins to a stop and leaves me undefended
Against the septic agony of wondering how-and-when ...
Sitting and flicking the parchments idly,
I hear the whole wild grief of autumn weeping,
Weeping for lost summers beyond the lost horizons,
Weeping with the torture of this alien world.

INTERLUDE IN WINTER

Pitching my curses at this stifling winter,
The dull dead missiles splash and splutter
Against the girders of the bourgeois mind.
The curses rain on an empty, aimless city,
Propped by the bobs and bows of marionettes.

O where are you going, my pretty maid,
And what, my lad, are you after?
Ten more years and the devil's paid
But you'll have lost your laughter.

So the grim hatred surges for mid-winter,
Swings and smoulders with violent probe
For all the reckless cities of the heart.
We shall never die in winter, they say,
Though summer and winter die in us.

O why are you sobbing, my pretty maid,
And why does the boy gape in sorrow?
Ten more years and the devil's paid,
Though neither may see tomorrow.

A little time for staring in the sun,
For watching clouds sail in a vacant sky ...
And then? And then the purpose that is ours
Shall burgeon from more fertile soil,
Where falls the feathery spray in spring.

O why are you singing, my pretty maid,
And why is the lad out of mourning?
Are the ten years up? Is the devil paid?
Is he off to hell in the morning?

SPRING 1943

And now the prisoned year has burst
The relentless circle of the seasons' spin:
And life is warm on lips in hedgerows,
Warm with the year's accumulated lust.

Spring's over there! And the frigid grate
No longer hungers for the crackling earth's decay;
Spring of the daffodils, offensives, chills—
And a girl in Sunday's park to greet.

Raids on Munich and Essen, we read,
Hearing the heavy pound and punch of bombs
Falling in parabolas like tipsy boulders ...
Revenge is audible but left unsaid.

Raid on the heart, *putsch* of spring,
The sand is falling and the dizzy mind
Registers its dumb protest—O sweet, mad life
The fertile mountains and the free birds sing!

LOVERS AT EVENING

From this uneven hill the grey world toppling
Cowers from the sloping pricks of rain.
This evening, needles jump on granite crags,
Falling around the neck and shoulders.
He never knew that she could knit
Her fine-boned scraps of beauty for his sake,
Or eat for him sour exile grass on Madigan.
So he, prouder than ten thousand blazing angels,
Stands in a cool dream and hears loudly
Her emotional tides forcing against his flanks,
While on the green ice of the flat lough
The seagulls pirouette like stumbling twigs:
And he, prouder than many-jewelled Indian princes,
Lips the glad wine bursting from heart to vein.

His girl is smiling through the muslin rain,
And can each moment coin the loving mood again.

THE MAIDEN AND THE MATRON

She grew as a star grows, as a flower forms,
Bright and shapely, in a cottage filmed by foliage:
Her food was simple and her singing soul
Was ignorant of fear and the curve of sorrow at the heart.

Her island was the white land of simple love,
Curled between the inland seas of purity and hope.
Her eyes had seen no ocean ships and her thoughts
Ran wild with the whip-muscled mountain sheep.

And so, the poet in you will see her limpid eyes,
And the honey river of her hair, the blackberry lips,
The free and passionate innocence of her
Who bathed for twenty years in flashing pearl-lit inlets.

And you will see the opening and closing of all things,
The maiden flower run to frightening fat ...
But you must close your worldly-waking eyes
And only see the creature with the singing soul.

THE BIRD

I

A bird flew tangent-wise to the open window.
His face was a black face of black, unknowing death.
His eyes threw the grim glint of sharpened stones,
That children pile by unfrequented roads.

And that night, dreaming into a rapture of cardboard life,
I started at the lean face of the bird:
A crow I think it was; but it was also death
And sure enough there was the crisp telegram next morning.

I placed my mirror to the flat, unfiltered light,
But the razor cut me, in spite of the guarantee,
And I knew it was not the razor, but the ebony beak
That slashed the base of my left nostril.

II

I loved the man who lay in the cheap coffin.
It was he first showed me the damp, stereoscopic fields
Of County Down; and now he was away to farm
The curving acres of his jealous God.

I loved the ploughing of his sun-caught brow,
And the hay-lines, and chicken-feathers in his hair
That was hay itself; the strongly cobbled boots,
And the swaying, coloured idiom of his mind.

And now he was lying with the Holy Bible under his chin,
Sorry only to have died before harvest and turf-cutting:
Lying dead in the room of rafters, and the grey, stopped clock—
Because of the hatred of the bird I did not kill.

III

Sometimes now, years after, I am nakedly afraid in mid-winter,
And ashamed to be afraid of an incessant beak
That raps a symphony of death on the window-panes
Of the window I dare not throw wide open.

But one evening, just before I go to bed to die,
There will be the black face of black, unknowing death,
Flying past my open window; there will be the black bird
With poison in his beak, and hatred in his wings.*

CYCLING TO DUBLIN

for Leslie Gillespie[*]

Pulling the dead sun's weight through County Meath,
We cycled through the knotted glass of afternoon,
Aware of bright fog in the narrow slot of breath,
And the cycles' rhyming, coughing croon.

O hurry to Dublin, to Dublin's fair city,
Where colleens, fair colleens are ever so pretty,
O linger no longer in lumbering languor,
Gallop the miles, the straight-backed miles without number.

We were the Northmen, hard with hoarded words on tongue,
Driven down by home disgust to the broad lands and rich talk,
To the country of poets and pubs and cow-dung
Spouting and shouting from every stalk ...

O hurry to Dublin, to Dublin's fair city,
Where colleens, fair colleens, are ever so pretty,
O linger no longer in lumbering languor,
Gallop the miles, the straight-backed miles without number.

MEMORIES OF DUBLIN

November 1940

The clean rectangles of many windows
And the sparkle of cheap jewellery.
All the colours of all spectrums ...
Flaring from the roof-line many

Restaurants and theatres burn
Signs of opulence and cynical good trade.
Jabbing inhuman spears they turn
Shannon's virility on passing faces.

Clashing coloured life and gaiety,
Dirt and yells, and the shrill suspense
Of empty alley-ways; Blackpool lights; cooking smells.
All this in past or future tense.

The façades of the eighteenth century—
Burke and Goldsmith frozen for posterity,
Who whistle and spit near culture's sanctuary
And drawl opinions on an isolated war.

Broad, glowing pavements, damp
With stout spittle, and soft Dublin rain;
Halitosis; an experienced, scented vamp:
Snatches of doggerel on the tongue.

The city is so much scenery from the Abbey:
The people are waxen marionettes.
For them, the rush for drinks and shabby
Buses; then nausea, dull, bottled joy in heart.

ULSTER

Ulster is firm and gaunt and black ...
Her stripes of hollow fields are ribs
That stare at the grey-splashed sky;
She is coarse and ungrateful,
And her dark men have heavy speech
—Deliberate speech, harsh and slow—
Belying the latent passion
Of unsuspected Celtic blood.

And Ulster is the mother-symbol
Of stolid, stupid sordidness?

Ulster's soul is tense with beauty
—Wild, curtained beauty
Bursting in fierce reticence,
Old and grim like basalt,
Yet fresh in day's caress.

Standing under the wing of gantries,*
The phallic sentinels of Belfast's lough,
He ponders beneath pride's vacant sneer,
Hating and loving futile majesty.

BELFAST

30 January 1942

Stranded here on this archipelago of winter
The evil wind swirls in the sail, and the bitter soil
Is hot and heavy to the hand that fondles.
Guard from fever, fret, infection the fervent fire
That streams its whiteness, like a maddened headlight tossing
On a copper sea, locked fast as mercury in palm.

THE FAR COUNTRY

There is a far country where there is a hall for dreams
And the taut hopes of men who have sweated in the sun,
You will find a lake for cooling and for healing
The jibes and bruises of the dour machines.

It is no country for School Captains, healthy thinkers,
Men with salt-and-pepper minds, ribbons on their hearts;
Only for the hungry and halt and humbled
Do these white switchback lanes, those careless meadows open ...

Over there no one shall seek escape and no one
Shall break in agony or bend under the unjustified load,
Over there all may swim in the lake of cooling
And sins peel off as slimy film from skeleton.

There in the far country there is a niche for dreams,
But not for going and getting, or praying and petting,
But you will find no salt in the lake that is not lacking
And life will peel away, will fall and wither and peel away.*

THE POET ANSWERS

Come, take a warning from the violent times
When the cock crows death in the early light
Flinging his scarlet comb to the big red sun.
And the blood-drops clutch to rusted wire,
And bombers drone home to their hives of terror,
Back over the smoking chimneys from blazing docks
With wings singed by hatred or delivered duty.
The poet guarding the fragrance of surrendered pasts,
Watches our faith slither to hell one fine morning:
And the poet thinks of the sterile critic, of the common man,
Of their shared contempt of the personal vision,
Of the propagandist sliding rulers of metric value.
Write, they will say, write of the political struggle,
We have no interest in your faint and copulative heart,
Revived in rhyme to make a needless measure.
And the answer is plain, the answer shouts itself.
Comrades, listen comrades, the poet speaks in his turn:

I am I, I am the poet, the maker, the breaker,
I am the prophet, the madman, the dreamer, the healer,
I am the killer, the killed, the universal panacea
For the broken, the inarticulate, the oppressed, the tortured.
I make—therefore I am! I make!
Myself is a every man, my wounds are all wounds,
My hopes are for all classes, colours, creeds,
My love beckons across the mountainous continents
Of fear and evil, over the indifferent swamps.
My world is all the world, all worlds,
My agony is the agony at Calvary and Dachau.
The echoes of the poet's words make urgent thunder
Against the ignorant critics and the scornful men.
The poet answers them all with his humble arrogance:
Searching for the Christ in me, I know my hollowness.

I am no banker, comrades, no politician, no diplomat,
No speculator in the sprawling greed of my fellows:
I only watch the great moon turning somersaults
Or see the leaping grains of rain blown by wind
Through an afternoon in late April, while leaves twitch ...
I am nothing but the flame in me, nothing, nothing,
And yet I am all things from rain streaming down panes
In basement kitchens where the faded delph is cracked
And mice run over the disused smells of cupboards,
To the driving whiteness of Niagara in flood,
And the ripe tang of August corn in Irish meadows,
And the brown smile of a country girl taken in love,
Whose hair veers towards the swallow-laden South ...

I am I, I am the poet, I am the maker
Whose testament is scribbled on a million hearts!

POEM WRITTEN IN SEPTEMBER

Now in September, while trees are continent though tired
From summer's steam and the storm-wet days of last August,
Now in the soiled end-paper of the season's book
It is opportune to add the double-column entries,
Balance the accounts of reason, faith and sentiment.
Tot up the afternoons of warmth and moisture,
The chance meeting with the beautiful and plain,
To eye in retrospect the talk in railway carriages,
The tennis elbow and the pilgrimage for chocolates,
To view the ragged peaks of loveliness,
The fevered graph of fervid sirens.
Perhaps one too should speak of love?
But love is too magic and too precious,
Too intangible, too difficult, too easily lost ...
Rather, the khaki strokes of lorries in the streets,
That run into the tapestry of total war,
And the search for individual responsibility,
And the conscious lack of integration.
Where has leaped the faith of that September,
When black-outs were expensive novelties,
When resolution flowed in flowering cascades?
Still, in the last curve of faith's circle,
There is little tarnished brightness,
There springs a sullen spark to fire.
Now in September, while trees are clothed and continent,
Before they strip for winter's bitterness,
In the crushed end-paper of this season's book,
Write off the score, revise the notes, correct the proofs,
For now it is opportune to add the double-column entries.

from

THE UNDYING DAY

(1948)

NOTHING REMAINS, NOTHING ALTERS

Nothing remains, my dear, and nothing alters.
The end of the eagle's flight leads back to the same
Dull, intrepid journey through the known wind passages
Although he flies to different places,
Eyeing new scrolls of landscape and former vistas
Unerringly different as the different climates of love.
The airman's aim is vicarious, he plunders from command:
The young avenging robot of decaying age,
Removed safe distances from the fevered air of action.
His landscape unravels out to planned destruction.
But neither eagle nor airman, intent on purposes,
Can wed tense minute to its eager fellow
Stretching them all into a circling mile of minutes
Crammed with the white energy of vaulting youth.
Can ever lovers' soldered lips remained enthralled
For one long tremulous day on end?
Or can the fire in her eyes flash heat
To warm the drab heart into passion every winter?
Nothing remains, my dear, nothing alters
The flight from love, the flight again to love ...
O let us always tend this garden of twin joy
Hunted by the old recurrent fears in never splendid places.

SEPTEMBER RETURNS

September returns without the usual bitterness,
Without the hostile witnesses briefed against me
In the year's courtmartial, demanding reparation,
Threatening the calm richness glossing summer.
And if the stain of bitterness has been erased
From off the workings of the heart's deep mine,
Thanks fly in squadron tiers across the months
To her who placed herself between the grief and me,
Holding my crystal hopes tight and unfaltering,
Knowing them with that woman's sure instinct
(I learned it slowly, graceless and alone).
Through all those months now gummed in the memory
She moved with freedom's joy, loving them all,
Embroidering my days with coloured splendour,
And covering up my armour's gaping crevices.
What can one salvage from those tender mornings
Tinted with affection, mid-day's sun strenuous
To one who never quite could trust the sun:
Afternoon still and fixed as grandfather's wedding group,
Evening confident, lovely as trees in Chinese print?
Sometimes walking leaf-fallen paths among the trees
I found her penetrate my mind, so warm and free,
Or by sea's phosphorescence, in the night air,
When the lights, pin-pointed, dazzled and danced,
There fell a rapturous, glowing peace
That tingled later in a sweet surprise
That all this could be so, and was:
Or when our bodies clenched, to match our minds,
When all the world slept right and purposeful,
(The incandescent flame cut through the barrier,
Lighting the last dark isolation corridor).
O then this damp, catarrhal earth was justified!
And in our island fortress, love's brave bastion,

We still remembered those who craved for unity
They could not find: we once had known that dry despair.
We saw the ghostly people of our splendid world
Dribbling inside the terror-riven castles,
And yet we still believed in swift, anonymous morning
Sun-speared and beautiful beyond our adolescent dreams,
More beautiful because of watches in the charnel night,
And the jetsam littering the abandoned shore.
By the sad pools and fern-freckled woods we pondered
Silently and tiptoed to that secret world of youth
Where nothing dies and every bird's a phoenix.

FALLING

This autumn the leaves fall fast
—O it won't be the last, don't worry—
But the quivering heart has passed
Its first zenith.

 Red-gold, crisp-brown, they curl on ground
—August-parched in those no-rain days—
And they are trampled in crackling sound
Monotonously.

So the year's been put on pension
—Half-pay has no emotion—
It's the end of pretension
Winterwalking.

The man prefers the year's fall
—While the poet's shadow eavesdrops, silhouetted—
Each must carry his own pall
While foot falters.

Fine days, wet days, days coloured, days plain
—Thousands shall fall, right hand, left hand—
Soon we'll hear the bright litany again
At winterend.

POEM TO K.D.

I send you greetings, Kay,* now in this exiled time
From this careless Augustan city of grace and slums,
Where in Merrion Square the whispers of death
Gauze over the rhododendrons and the parched grass.
I greet you from a neutral country in a neutral hour
When the blood pace slows and nothing stirs
But the leaves in the parks, so gently:
So gently that not even the newspaper headlines
Can fluster the plumes of swans, gliding, gliding,
As on a lake of fire, fringed by pink water.
The pulse of life is faint, as in a trance,
As we await the backwash of hate's last outrage.
All Europe's continent pivots, for me, in Stephen's Green:
Your Warsaw and Normandy fester in happy Hampstead,
Cupped in a shell of gentleness, withdrawn from the terror
That, fevered with swift desire, strides beyond our barricades ...
But everywhere we see the uncharted darkness melt,
We see the sun pour on the sap-drained faces,
The oil of joy press motion in the wheels of love,
The masks fall off, the undying day return!

LINES FOR FRIENDS

In the soiled days, thin and obsolete as Queen Victoria pennies,
He walks, like a brass rod, searching for his Madonna flower,
Towering the image of their still-sealed child across the trees,
Soldering his introspection to the daily struggle.

Where sweep the red and green and gold, plant and grass
    and bark,
Swerving bank on bank, flat forest on sunken forest,
Dressed in a brittle suit, he steps at the edge of life,
Cautiously, being uncertain of being and begetting.

And she is silent, stiff as bronze snake in a sterile room,
Her hands perplexed in pain between the yellow sheets,
Feet are dancing on the skylight and in the womb.
She remembers the sensuous delights in early spring

When by centre, body on body falling
With swift and animal but always gentle wish,
This present pain was made with the tall man
Who taught her joy to jig from earth to love's bright planet.

Deep in the crowded wood on this dim day
The pools throw frost-edged eyes that blink and grin ...
Whin* and thistle and the weeds of a wan winter
You are fit symbols for this time of tearing war

—For a time of death and the compassing of birth,
For the girl in labour, who can so lovingly pretend ...
My friend, with head so angular and firm and proud,
A poet sends his greetings for your Christmas child.

SPEECH BEFORE WINTER

It comes again. The spin to the year's end
Circles to its last full stop. I defend
The fires of autumn that purr on the ground,
The stacked-up leaves, the twitching gusts that sound,
The drawn silences here in this island,
Where the slant and pace of life are still bland.
The autumn swerves with equable pulse,
But summer eyes have turned from joy long since,
O what's the use of limping sentiment,
That crinkles the shell of my still content,
Who am more free when the great winds are loose,
More free when frames of mind restrict my choice?
Wandering winterward as vagrant leaf,
Without the saving grace of hope or grief,
All my aloneness blossoms into pain,
Plots on my pattern's rim another stain.
Come, let me end this chapter: let me close
The dog-eared chronicle that spites repose!
Exile from love's the only bitterness,
That gives this unmanned heart its trembling guess.
O what's the use of limping sentiment,
That wrinkles the shell of my smooth content.

MICHAEL WALKED IN THE WOOD

Michael walked in the green wood
With his friends in buzzing summer
And they talked economics
And art in the clover.

To animal noises of secretive woodland
Michael was listening between the grim strictures.
In the grey-blanket sky pebbled with blue
One voice sang in sad pictures—

'Like a leaf in the city wind
Brief man is blown
From pavement to pavement
In drab discontent.

'Like a petal he falls
On the river's fake silver,
Soundless he perishes
Without a farewell.

'Like a tree in a storm
His roots are struck out
And the grass ever-cunning
Firms down the torn earth.

'Like a leaf in a city September
He eddies and eddies.
Brief man is blown
From pavement to pavement ...'

Michael talked in the green wood
With his friends in their summer
And they walked as they talked
Among ferns and bracken and clover.*

SANDYMOUNT

The water-drifts at Sandymount
Stretch like dazzling spears of light,
Across the foreshore acreage
Like little streaks of wild delight.

Tripping across the tawny sand
Canary-costume with an escort walks,
Keeps her sniffing dog in tow
And in an offhand manner talks.

Her dog barks sharply, whirls and wheels
Prowls around the razor shells
Beside the lonely Martello tower,
Who walks alone no secret tells.

Islands of water gape and glare,
Clouded sky thumbs nose at elegance,
The talked-out couple quickly pace;
On Irish weather take no chance.

The water-drifts at Sandymount
Lie forlorn, with none to care,
Except the yelping, gleeful dog
That cannot find a desert there.

AUTUMN PRELUDE

The trees are battered sheets of bronze,
Whose rust lies powdered on the ground,
While near-by corn—thin rods of gold—
Stands fertile in the sun's glad stare;
The fields are speechless with content.
(Unfathomed overflow of joy,
That empties summer's canisters,
Weeps for their foliate sacrifice.)

And the road is a taut ribbon,
Whitely passive with the tangents
Of would-be hidden army vans,
Nurses and perambulators,
(A neutral ribbon typing out
The rise and fall in human stocks.)

The branches hang like wild questions,
And will an answer from the leaves
That lie in isolated pools ...
(The answer is the swishing of rubber,
Moving to arrest the motion
Of wheels and life, of all our race.)

CAUGHT

Everywhere, cold as neglected bones on Northern hills,
Wet as boots in bogs whose sore sponge squelches,
Brilliant as the half-lit glamour spraying neutral Dublin,
Cold and wet and brilliant she follows after everywhere ...
Lost in the deserted grasses swift flies the wish
To melt apart those unimpassioned eyes and stabbing lips,
To lose my own identity and stride anonymous
Through the spiral mist on mountain belly,
Where I could be more glad than lucid stream
Serenely walking free to ocean's tomb.
But wishing is not making, is hardly hopeful,
Finding her shadow running even into my stillness ...

O there's no holiday from love's white raging wheel!

SONG OF THE ODD, OLD MAN

I could tell you of odd, old dreams
Before the acid stirred in my blood,
I could tell you of talking hills
And the red splendour when the flood
Of the toppling world was young
And hope rang morning bells,
And no one had evil tongue,
Or crafty, leching eye—
And all was a strange, strange glory.
I was a poet then
Long before rhyming was,
Before the fissured glen
Echoed the golden word.
The magic that is man
Swung in the quivering pulse,
And the rivers leaped and ran
For the ecstasy of life ...
I could tell you of odd, old dreams
But then I'm an odd, old man
And even to me it seems
So very, very long ago.

SHORT STORY IN VERSE

'Well, my dear, it's like this
(After the most perfunctory kiss)
'I think your bloody politics
Are simply drawing-room tricks.
I mean ideals are all right,
But that won't help us fight
The Nazis'. He didn't understand her quite.

The numb sky spread like a barn roof,
Whose lead-ribbed parallels had lost their proof
Against the suave, insinuating streams
Of silk rain-water: and the path-lost beams
Of searchlights scored their taut, umbrella map,
When the girl surrendered to the chap
At the stone ditch: didn't give a rap.

'I had the comrades once', she thought,
'And did as a good girl ought,
Beneath ice-island eyes: but without fear
My sullen body falls to a man with fresh beer
On claimant lips. He's stupid, but so awfully nice ...
And I must have a man once or twice,
Before they slaughter them all like spring-torn mice'.

The sea ran loose at the fields' edge,
Throwing the dry, dun grass a pledge
Of damp days; and the sea's sore croon
Cringed below a piece of moon
As in love tales of modern times,
That tell themselves in almost rhymes,
Passion went leaping through the limes.

WAITING FOR SPRING

Waiting (Who knows why? Who cares?)
Or being restive for the live seed
Pushing the green stem sun-wards,
The earth's fertility is all one's joy:
Waiting for the evening's stream
Of rippled silence.
Through the young, unbroken fields
There sounds the tense, undying pulse,
The steady rapture of love-lying hills:
Waiting for the first shrill
Of cuckoo-chant,
The man's eyes hang the grey hedge-lines
With all the globes of fairyland:
Waiting on many lips of coast,
The white, flashing terror of the bayonets
Flies arrows to malignant sky:
But sky and earth are unaware of fear,
And heedless of the plummet joy,
The solemn menace of our spring.

DIALOGUE IN THE STORM

LEADER OF THE CROWD
Ring up the curtain, boys, we'll have a speech
From this mad fellow of the streets,
This poet wanderer who claims to gauge the inner soul,
The self-styled man of wisdom, But enough!
Let him tell his own story,
Defend his practices as best he can.

THE ARTIST
My friends, I shall begin immediately,
For the time has come to speak my piece,
Whoever may be offended or disturbed.
You see me here, poet against the common will,
A seeming parasite in labour-glorious hives.
According to the rules prescribed by the rabble
I am a failure, I—

VOICE OF THE CROWD
We won't be insulted, Mister poet,
We must have our rights and know it.
We'll pull you down for insolence!
Less of that self-satisfied pretence!

THE ARTIST
Please calm yourself. I mean no harm
To you or to your fellows here.

I am a failure, then, as the world thinks.
But each failure, as I think,
Is a new kind of success
And each success is a new kind of failure.
Speaking in paradoxes is speaking in truth,
For no truth is whole or absolute,

Just as no lie is always a lie.
And let me say in all earnestness
That hope and despair are both equivalents,
Pole opposites of the same mendacious coin,
Twelve-sided with iniquity and fear.

LEADER OF THE CROWD
So that's all you can say.
I'll tell you a better one, my hearties.
Listen to this and judge for yourselves—
A couplet I heard from a *real* poet.
(He told it over a pint of Guinness.)
Johnny went riding on a comet,
Fell down to earth, started to vomit.
There's a lesson in that for those that see it.
And humour too—that's well to the fore.

THE ARTIST
I shall unfold a little parable:
The wind rises everywhere and it soars
Over the cones of the grey-blue hills,
Above all minds and over the sharp pines.
And the frost comes roaring, black in winter,
To still the patterns of the magic woods.
The wind that flows at dawn is truth:
It blows to every corner, no one can stop it.
And in the frost is the spirit:
You will never crush the spirit,
For it is eternal and shall endure.
Let us ponder on these things.

CHORUS FROM THE CROWD
We're not convinced by any of that
Because it sounds too grand, too pat,
We want square meals and peace perhaps
And roofs to cover us normal chaps.
We want the things we can taste and touch
Our smokes and food and women and such,
And perhaps with a little security.
To the devil with futurity!

THE ARTIST
I shall come to the point you raise.
You say: Art is not life or food,
One can't live on paint and metre,
Or pay the rent with histrionics,
Or exchange surrealist drawings for bread,
Or even feed the cat on milkless rhythms.
But who ever thought it was otherwise?
Certainly no artist, who lives on social scraps,
By the indifference of the man in the street
And the grace of policemen on their beat,
Who sometimes protect him, sometimes fail.
I can assure you, it isn't the artist.

SECOND VOICE FROM THE CROWD
All right, we'll take your word for it,
Though we still have our doubts.
But what we want to know is this,
Can you make our lives any happier?

THE ARTIST
Well, if you give me time to explain,
Perhaps I'll show you what I mean.
Anyhow, I propose that the artist and the crowd
Should work out their destinies one with the other.
Otherwise we may both perish,
And the machine may grind over us.
You are all men, of similar make to me:
I claim no mystic superiority.
But your mistake is a common mistake,
Believed even by men of highest intellect,
Whose integrity cannot be impugned,
Happiness and goodness don't just consist
In filling your bellies and having intervals
Before starting to fill them again.
What better is such behaviour
Than that of those who are your taskmasters?

And unless all your hearts are pure
Is there any guarantee that such a system
Would continue indefinitely?
That one of your fellows might not become oppressor?
Selfishness is the great enemy:
When we destroy him, then the devil dies.
Selfishness is the most ugly giant.

LEADER OF THE CROWD
We are many, they are few,
But our hands are tied
So what shall we do?
Where's the artistic pride
In the face of injustice?
So what can we say or do?

THE ARTIST
I don't deny the urgency of the situation.
But, on the other hand, you underrate the difficulty.
You are deceived by the obvious,
That the barricades will lead to plenty,
That men in the mass act intelligently
Or are even stirred by common humanity.
All history denies the truth of this view
However unfortunate for the socially conscious.
You forget, too, of the seed of the spiritual
That lies wrapped deep in the hearts of the most ignoble
And of the necessity for following gods.
(Even deceitful gods are better than none.)
My prognosis is not an optimistic one
But a little reflection will prove it true.

CHORUS FROM THE CROWD
Tell us, tell us, show us the way,
Tell us what to do and say.

THE ARTIST
Even there you are wrong entirely.
Why should you swing over to my side
Without due consideration?
My advice to you is to separate,
Stop being a crowd, divide, be individual,
Try to think out a way for yourselves,
Refuse to believe what the preacher preaches,
Or what a man may argue over a drink.
Remember that each of you carries the world
Within his consciousness, that each of you
Is more important than the aggregate ...

CHORUS
We want the things we can taste and touch,
Our smokes and food and women and such.
When we've got a little security,
Then we'll think of futurity.

THE ARTIST
I see that you are getting restless
And are preparing to move off together.
I apologise if I have bored you,
Or have been unnecessarily rude.
But I do pray that you may consider
The few suggestions I have thrown you.
I can see the people everywhere lose their sameness,
Throw the manufactured opinions to the tides,
Lift in all the earth strong hands of brotherhood,
Commune with every man and bear his burden.
And on each forehead burn the flame
Of Christ, Whose Name is every Name.

CHORUS FROM THE DISTANCE
We are many, they are few,
Our hearts beat strong
And we'll try to do
What's good for each.

We are many, they are few
We'll win the day
When we're sure of what we do.

THE ARTIST
Yes, comrades, now you're speaking true
You'll win when you're sure of the things you do.
And the earth shall move in your hand,
And the earth shall live in your palm.

THE UNDISCOVERED ISLAND

FIRST VOICE
They seek an island in a hollow time,
They seek an island across the fringe from our time,
Removed across the fabulous golden mountains,
Beyond the counted continents, on, on, on ...
To where the cormorants live alone, perched on strong rocks.
They swing their compass to the miraculous west,
They move east to the dreamlands, south to the wheatlands,
They track ceaselessly to the arid north of resolution,
They follow the waves' roads from ocean to ocean,
For water is pure and contains the earth in its atom.
They fight their guerrilla battles tirelessly:
They thirst; but their flags are planted
On the sands that the tides conquer.
They find no island of delight.

MAN'S VOICE
I am a city clerk, I work from nine to six.
I know nice people, live a little beyond my means,
But watch the overdraft with cautious practised eye.
My neighbours are carefully chosen, almost professional, people
Who also live very slightly above their means,
Know an occasional artist, golf in winter, tennis in summer,
Make the seasons span with bridge parties,
Are kind to animals, keep all ideas in the ice-box,
Insure their existences, love no women but their wives
And are much too nice to speak of passion,
Except when it's frightfully the correct angle.
But sometimes, alone in the office with pencilled figures,
Dates and memoranda, doodled pads, telephone numbers,
I have heard the scream of spring, and summer's riot,
And autumn's oboe dirge: winter's long black finger

Has tapped the window—and joy once frightened me.
Or crawling upstairs on bus, better to view the passing show,
The legs of girls have sprung blood to the cheek,
And perfume has cricked my neck, discreetly at distance.
I remember ... But these are not the real things.
Life is real, earnest; like accounts, like bank balances,
Like the goods in the warehouse, like real estate,
Like indigestion and B.O. and the spear of rheumatism.
When I was a junior clerk I wrote verses to a pasty typist
But she seldom smiled across the crusted ledgers.
The island dissolved in a mist of frustration:
I no longer dream of the island ...
I no longer dream of its sights and sounds ...

WOMAN'S VOICE
The blistering cold of winter freezes thought
To a stiff jelly even in the brightest mind.
So seek those patterned lives where always life
Is free and glorious, where the winds are never rude.
But how shall we know that shimmering island
For a certainty: might we mistake
Its forest for the dross of painted scenery;
Might we mistake its mercury rivers
For silvered scratches on deceptive cloth;
Might we not fear the facile self-deception,
And the futile anger of the near-miss?
We do not know the infallible marks of the island,
How stand its trees or how the streamlets pulse,
We do not know ...

FIRST VOICE
Should one now attempt to adjust the response,
Or rehearse the subtle answer in the brain?
The solution will come, will assuredly come.
One shall reply from a dignified stance,
Refusing all that is slick and fake,
Challenging the syrup of the moist cinema,
Ready to jettison the easy justification.
When seeking that island, beyond the ocean of despair,
Live always only as for one day,
Be undismayed should they erect a cross,
Be ready to accept the necessary isolation.
Thus shall the island, proud, invincible,
Appear on the far horizon's coil.

THE GLORIOUS TWELFTH

12 July 1943

You will remember that the Twelfth was always dry,
That rain followed the day after, some said as Judgement,
While others argued that drums of Ulster stirring
Pulled out the corded wetness from our local skies.
Four years ago we heard them last, heard the thunder
Smouldering through the ribboned streets towards the battle
In the fields of Finaghy. There was fire then,
Fire in our throats, fire beaten out from our cities,
Cold, distant, strongly arid in the normal weather:
Four years ago since last we heard the drums' thunder,
Since the Orange banners looped in gay procession
And bands of flute and fife, of brass and silver
Played hell to the Pope and immortality to William—
To William, Prince of Orange, defender and avenger,
To William, the stiff Dutch Protestant who saved us
From villainous James, the tyrant Stuart King.

Remember 1690, remember the ancient wrongs of Rome,
Remember Derry, Aughrim, Enniskillen and the Boyne,
The Glorious Boyne in Ireland, where the Pope was overcome,
Remember the Maiden City and the breaking of her boom.

These were my people marching on the streets,
Released from inhibition and resolved to keep the faith.
Four years have passed since Ulster opened up her heart,
And toasted her deliverance from the Seven Hills,

Four years since fire has run swift rivers into Europe
From Dunkirk to Briansk, from Naples to Novgorod,
From Caucasus to Clyde, from Warsaw to Belfast.

And now, in Derry and Downpatrick, no Ulstermen are
    marching
To the rustle of their banners and the flogging of their drums.
Our red-brick cities have their blackened skeletons,
Our people carry the public and the personal wound.

Forgotten 1690, forgotten the ancient wrongs of Rome,
Forgotten Derry, Aughrim, Enniskillen and the Boyne,
The Glorious Boyne in Ireland where the Pope was overcome,
Forgotten the Maiden City and the breaking of her boom.

You will remember that the Twelfth was always dry,
While now in Italy the bloods of Continents are joined,
While now the Russian plains are stacked with corpses,
Rotting in the Red sun, feeding plagues to common rats ...
But after carnage there will be music, after death will be hope,
After the horror of the day will come the evening dream,
After hatred's harvest joy will march, shrouded, to Finghy.

LAMENT FOR FRANCE

All, all is fallen now, fallen and flouted.
All the bridges are mined, all the flags are withered,
All the frontiers are twisted back, all the faces
Have become the one face, the gigantic face of terror.
('Nothing will stop us now', say the feet,
'Down are the barriers. Nothing stands in the way!
What do they say—do they say "Liberty"?
My truncheon, Hans, that's the answer to freedom!')
On the boulevards there are only the dead leaves,
Falling, falling, before the appointed season:
In the heart there is only the black knock of fear
That thumps unceasing sordid thunder,
('What do they say, Fritz?—what's this equality?
So men are equal! The equality we respect
Is that of the steel arm, the knuckleduster fist ...
That's our equality! Death to the Jews!')
Everywhere they are taking down the symbols of France!
The people speak in the whisper and gesture of death,
Eyes drained of meaning, tongues dry with despair.
O what have we done, O what is our crime?
('They say that men are brothers! They'll be brothers all right.
Brothers at the abattoir! You like my joke, Friedrich?
We'll teach them a new humour ... Where's my whip?')
They will take everything—yes, everything
That can be assessed, all that will be taken.
They will smash down pity and loveliness, trample them down.

They will kill and plunder, break and ravish,
They will do these things: nothing can stop them now.
On the boulevards the crisp leaves are mourning,
Weeping for all that is fallen before its due season.
In the heart, the only flow is the trickle of hope
Which cannot be commandeered like the lorries or cattle.

In the heart, the Republic lives beyond her death
Till grave-faced men shall bring the phoenix-birth.
Where brothers shall be equal, proudly free,
They will remember France, salute her memory.

NIGHT IN DUBLIN

January 1944

Stand easy now, while the world spins: look inward,
See yourself walk stammering towards the heart's defeat;
Watch the last surrender of the vagrant lamps,
Each ebbing, flowing into unregenerate night.
We are the defeated: all men are the defeated,
Especially the conquerors—they are the most defeated.
Especially the man who finds ambition's terminus,
Especially those who lived without perilous aim,
Who dribbled out their little lives in safe retreats—
All these are of the dark conquered.
And what of those who lived beneath the unhalting shadow,
Whose wounds were newly-salted day marching on day?
What of those who clung to their small living
Not because of any quality of life
But because they feared to think of death?
(O sweet annihilation, bride and mistress ...)
Were they all too of that defeated class?
No one answers the insistent bell,
No doors swing open into radiant halls,
No footsteps clatter on the uncarpeted stairs ...
Choose a bright morning for your questioning:
Sun still is sure although the night be obdurate.

THE KINGDOM SHALL COME

The chords of emotion mutter,
The leaves of intellect brown,
But nothing now can splutter
Save the rains that amble down.

The vigorous thigh may pester
And blood spill into the sea,
Or hope may suckle to fester,
And the apples rot on the tree.

The earth may bathe in the splendour
Of men gone murdering men,
While agnostics shall defend her
Against the priests' 'Amen!'

In the week when our seed shall wonder
And the roots of the hate be numb,
At the crinkle of fervent thunder,
The Kingdom shall whistling come.

from

A GARLAND FOR
CAPTAIN FOX

(1975)

RUNE AND BLADE

Soldiers take pride in saluting their Captain,
Where are the captains that govern mankind?

from 'A Full Moon in March' by W.B. Yeats

Fox stamps on our undemanding age,
Preferring what's ordained, exact,
Shaped to its mould by ancient use.
He argues for the rule of captaincy
That must remain though kings depart;
Not least affirms the magic art
That comes from maker's stoic trade
And blesses custom, ritual, ceremony,
Upheld by rune and lustrous blade.

CAPTAIN FOX

Captain Fox sits reading metaphysics—
Hegel's the hundred watt bulb in his world.
Captain Fox is fond of Zürich's Hotel Excelsior.
'A reliable place', he says, 'Solid, reliable'.
He lights a Gauloise* and blows a ring:
'One of these days I'll retire, I'm getting too old
For buggering along the autobahns.
Besides, I want to write a pre-Ayer* work on philosophy
Which I'll publish at my own expense.
Aspects of Hegel or some such title.
Perhaps a village on the Adriatic ...'

Basques, Catalans, Slovaks, Irishmen, Blacks,
These are Captain Fox's friends
Or perhaps, more exactly, business associates.
Luckily he's as much linguist as philosopher.
He talks for hours about fireworks
And the poetry of Rainer Maria Rilke.
Truly a civilised man, Captain Fox.

'Are you in business?' I once asked him.
'Well, let's say I provide ... facilities'.
A most civilised man, Captain Fox,
Discreet, solid, reliable.

His business isn't my business.

THE LETTER

There it was one morning, lying flat in the hallway,
An elegant square envelope with a Uruguayan stamp.
I turned it over and read 'Fox' and an unknown address.
I smiled that in the end each coin spins true,
That dead bones are fleshed in the sun,
That the heart sings out its zany tune.
But then, before opening the letter, I sensed a trick
For mind, heart-hating, never sings,
Is vigilant for enemies, insults, disappointments.

I tore the letter open. *Yes yes yes yes yes.*
Heart's confidence vindicated. Doubt only the mind.

'Like Mark Twain's, greatly exaggerated ...
Getting into a rut ... need to start a new life ...
Contemplation not action ... regret hasty departure ...
Bored with Switzerland ... my 'double', poor chap ...
Attempt to frame me ... importance of friendship'.

I hope to see Montevideo before I die.

AN ERRAND, A PROMISE

Don't ask why he sent me a registered parcel.
Inside there was a brief note, a book token and a sealed envelope.
'Please deliver personally. My best thanks. Cordially, F.'
The bulging envelope was addressed to someone at the F.O.—
Well, the name was Carrington-Smythe, if that means anything.
I took it round by taxi and got a receipt
Which I airmailed without delay to Montevideo.
Errands for the Captain are done speedily, lovingly.
I bought the revised *Chambers Dictionary* with the token;
Captain Fox likes his friends to keep improving their minds.

Did I hear a murmur: 'What game's the old boy playing at now?'
Frankly, I don't know and I'd advise you not to ask.
But eventually I'll write the official *Life*
As crammed with pearl point notes as an insurance policy.
The shut doors will slide open,
There'll be a gathering of hard facts.
Captain Fox will be de-mythologised at last.

NOTES TOWARDS THE
FOX BIOGRAPHY

Born in Cologne, 1920, father a Sergeant-Major
Serving in the British Army of Occupation;
Mother from Banbridge, Co. Down, Pop. (1926) 5,000.
Youngest of the family, knew German before English,
Schooled throughout the British Isles without distinction
But nevertheless won an Exhibition to Oxford;
Never went near Cowley-cum-Dreaming-Spires
Because of some youthful love entanglement.

Joined the Army at Dad's suggestion,
But heard no angry shot in World War II,
Became an 'Army intellectual' but could hold his own
At the outdoor pursuits of the upper classes.
Quickly assimilated officer class attitudes,
Soon promoted father to the rank of Major,
Seldom at a loss for answers to tricky questions.
Married a rich widow who died three years later.
Desk-bound, left the Army out of sheer boredom
But found the 'Captain' handle useful in business.

Business? Ah, that's something I must research.
Occasional frantic journeys, exchange of sealed envelopes.
Entertains mostly in hotel suites, no money worries.

I hope one day to fill these gaps.

NOT BURIED IN HIS SKIN

When the fox is dead his skin is sold,
If he lives long he will grow old;
Living he lives and dying he dies.
He is not buried in his skin, all honour to him!

The Captain first heard this riddle in Cologne
And how young Goethe played 'Dying Fox' in Sesenheim.
They put the candle out, its wick still glowing,
Then passed it round as they sat beside the large tiled stove
In the parsonage, a day's drive from Strasbourg.

Take the candle, quickly say the incantation, pass the candle.
Then when the glow dies out the one left holding the candle
Must pay the forfeit. On cheeks 'loveliest rosy red'
Goethe often planted a kiss. Sweet Friederike,
Blue-eyed in a short skirt with its black taffeta apron,
Light-footed as a deer. To be rejected but never forgotten.

Once, Fox recalls, the poet's eyes and face
Were scorched by a burst of flame. 'The fox', wrote Goethe,
'Was found to be not dead but very lively'.

Many a lady, like Friederike at her young love,
Has watched the uncommitted Captain go.
'I went, you stood, your eyes cast earthwards,
You watched me long with tear-filled eyes'.

The Captain, despite reports, is still not buried in his skin.
Living he lives, his skin unsold, all honour to him!

CAPTAIN FOX ON J. EDGAR HOOVER

G-man extraordinary, super-cop, crime-buster
With the pug face and four bullet-proof Cadillacs;
Snooper on public figures in private suites,
Flailer of deviates, sacker of G-Men
Who failed to observe the regulation haircut,
He never married but lived with Mom
Till she died when he was in his forties.
England should remember how he loved dogs.
Top Good Guy who licked the Baddies,
He was society's spiked fist.

Let's call his register of enemies:
George 'Machine Gun' Kelly, Ma and Pa Barker,
'Baby Face' Nelson, Alvin Karpis,
Frederick Duquesne, Julius and Ethel Rosenberg,
Harry Gold, Colonel Abel, the Brinks gang,
Hauptmann and Joe Valachi,
Dillinger and 'Pretty Boy' Floyd.*

His life was lived for Bad Guys:
Kidnappers, robbers, extortionists, traitors,
Jostling for their name in history
Like any President or poet or Attorney General.
The spur's a footnote in some mammoth book,
Nothing so vulgar as a hundred grand.

Said Lyndon Baines Johnson:
'I'd rather have him inside the tent peeing out
Than outside peeing in'.

Said Richard Nixon to the ageing G-Man:
'I want to discuss retirement'.
And Mr. America replied:
'Ridiculous. You're still a young man'.

This is the picture then, within whose frame
You see the Good Guys and the Bad.

The trick is knowing which is which.

KNOWING AND NOT KNOWING

Those who speak know nothing.
Those who know are silent.
These are the words of Lao-Tsu,
The sage who fathered Chinese Taoism.
The loquacious Captain often quotes them;
Someone once laughed when he recalled them.

The Captain smiled, gargled with his brandy.
'Ah yes', he answered lazily, 'now let me tell you
Of another Chinese, Po Chu-I of the T'ang dynasty.
Ever heard of him? No, I thought not.
Well, Po wrote a poem about Lao
And what he said was roughly this—
If indeed Lao-Tsu really knew
Why did he write a book about his knowledge?'

Nobody spoke for ages.

MIDWINTER, W.11.

Dragging afternoon in W. 11.—cardboard sky, pink westerly;
Holland Park Avenue's treetops like dark lacework
Or witches' brooms upended in the flat grey light;
Dogcrap, litter, a film of damp on the pavements,
The down-at-heel streets of a decayed Empire,
The ebb and flow of phlegmatic traffic,
The slim London vowels of children loosed from school;
A blind man's stick pecks the zebra crossing.

Observe the Captain driving a Volvo up Campden Hill Road
Towards the terrace on the brow, near where the water
tower stood
Before the speculators flailed it down in search of profit.
He carries a smart document case in Spanish leather
And rings the bell of a violet-doored, chic residence.
Carrington-Smythe of the F.O. lets him in, unspeaking.

Then two hours pass till Fox emerges, waves a goodbye.
Carrington-Smythe resumes his call to No. 10.
GOVERNMENT MAY FALL trumpets the *Evening Standard*,
But Fox has cooked the Opposition's goose
And steers his way westward into the stripling night.

TIME WINDS DOWN

The Captain sits with an open book
Mozart serenely warms the room

Time winds down

He turns the page of antique wove
The clock is sounding tick by tock

Time winds down

Sips brandy from a rounded glass
Faintly pencils in a note

Time winds down

Knows that a gunman in a mac
Might force the door and speed the shot

Time winds down

Slump the Captain on the floor
Soak the book with Fox's blood

Time winds down

Calm he sits and reads and sips
Mozart permeates the room

Time winds down

FOX ASLEEP

Fox sleeps naked in a starlet's arms
Freed from angst and night's alarms

River spilled in ocean wide
Drawn by swift ecstatic tide

Into what meadows will he wander
Dawdling hither, rushing yonder?

Are his images of bliss
Cooling water, loved one's kiss?

Ghosts of innocence or guilt?
At what windmills will he tilt?

Or in fields of white delight
Does he dreamwalk through the night?

Let the sleeping Captain lie
Till day restores urbanity.

from

YOUNG MR. GIBBON

(1979)

RATS

Captain Fox's dinner party was under way
In a private room at the Savoy.
His guests included an actor knight,
Carrington-Smythe of the F.O. and a chemist
Who was talking, between bites of salmon,
About morphine addiction in rats.
'This is paralleled', he was saying, 'by an increase
In the amount of encephalin in their brains.
You see ...' Suddenly a waiter scurried in:
'Captain Fox, Sir, a man ... he says ...'

Then in the doorway loomed a figure,
Heavy and masked, a revolver in his hand.
'I've come for Fox', he growled.
All except Fox jumped to their feet.

'Then you'd better have a drink', said Fox,
'Everyone here is civilised'.
He started to pour another glass
But, lightning-quick, the bottle smashed
Into the dark intruder's face.
A shot rang out quite harmlessly,
Then Fox aimed straight for the groin.

The gunman sagged, fell to the floor
Like a sack of flour, moaning, dripping blood.
Fox hurried to the phone, his guests unfroze.

When the dinner resumed, Fox merely said:
'Pity to waste that St. Julien 1970'.
Then, turning to the pharmacologist:
'Now tell us more about the rats'.

BANKERS' SKY

A brute of a day it was
With rain flogging the pavements
The gutters flushing angrily
Towards the Zürichsee
The sun tiptoed out shyly
So we could glimpse
Gold helmets on the Grossmünster.

Having drunk to Fox's memory
Dozed to inert speeches
Wiped away hot tears
We stumbled in deep macintoshes
To the Seefeldquai.

James Joyce was mentioned
Somebody quoted from his 'Bahnhofstrasse':
'The eyes that mock me sign the way
Whereto I pass at eve of day'.

After that, another downpour
A real bugger of a day.

Solid Protestant city
Of numbered bank accounts,
Of Zwingli and C.G. Jung
Ghosted by Leopold Bloom and Lenin
Even its bankers' sky
Cries out the death of Captains.

CAPTAIN FOX'S DESERTION

Like Yeats, he deserted us in the stripling year,
Null mid-winter after the ancient festival.

Ground frost salted the roads
That joined nowhere to nowhere.

He would have sniggered at the obituaries,
Paper columns propping a marble reputation.

'Routine's the enemy', he used to say,
'Activity cancels out boredom,

Is a surrogate for commuting, family ties,
The Friday booze-up, the package holiday'.

Now he's gone, fewer things will happen,
Ennui will gnaw like a barn-rat.

But memory, like a trawler's net,
Rakes in its quivering shoal.

MEMORIES OF A DREAM

I hollered from the ironwork balcony: 'Captain! Captain!'
But the razored lawn was wordless, figureless.
Ten-nine-eight-seven-six and the Captain's ex-batman, Jack,
    materialised,
Sour as the bloody devil; and his girlfriend Margaret,
Naked, except for dark glasses. She dragged a trunk.
Together we humped it up the steps, no thanks to Jack.

In the house: waxed flowers under glass, green baize tables,
Peaches in hall-marked dishes, C.P. Scott's portrait.
Two unknown men in shirtsleeves and braces drinking Beaujolais
At the open window. A stuffed black bird on the carpet.
Words floated: 'Chomsky', 'paratoxic'.

A little old man came sidling in and said: 'I'm Freud'.
'Who has been zeeing zis Captain Fox?
I am wanting him for to analyse'.
Nobody answered but I knew the Captain
Was skulking, unanalysed, inside the trunk.
Jack and Margaret were coupling earnestly.
The oracle of Cross Street crashed from the wall.
London Bridge was falling down, falling, falling
Down on Sweeney and Mrs. Porter in the spring.

Freud muttered: 'To ze wrong house have I come'.
I shrugged, then offered him a peach.

DEGAS ON TALENT

The Captain enjoys remembering Degas on talent:
'Anyone can have talent when he is twenty-five,
The thing is to have it when you're fifty'.

Twenty-five, fifty: polished rounded figures,
Multiples of five, bland as rubbed pebbles.
The Captain at twenty-five, a supple figure
Who had moved elegantly through Hitler's war.
Fox in 1945, on tiptoe for adventure,
A T.E. Lawrence searching for his Arabia.
The Captain making points at the War Office,
Tenacious, untemperamental, never servile.
Fox tactfully rejecting his Colonel's lady.
Fox striding along the Kurfurstendamm.

The Captain in 1970, fifty not out,
Figure still lithe, face coarser, plumper,
Suited clubman-wise, regimentally tied,
A flattering portrait in the Summer Academy,
Still his own man but seen with celebrities
Strolling laughingly to his Pall Mall Club.
Fox the link-man, in touch with numerous capitals.
Fox the fixer, go-between extraordinary
(After a weekend at Chequers, a flight to Washington),
Fox as genial and inscrutable as ever.

Fox at fifty, twice as creative as at twenty-five,
No talent buried in the earth.

CRITICS AND PUBLISHERS

'Critics and publishers rarely spot the truly new
But fall for oldie crap and trendy gimmicks'.

—That's what Fox told me at his Club.
I pressed for an example.
Here's what he told me, word for word:

'Well, everybody knows of Joyce's drawn-out agony,
So I'll take instead the case of Malcolm Lowry,
Dipso and genius, still not wholly recognised.
I met him in Vancouver and a few times down in Mexico
Soon after Hitler's war; poor Malc was seldom sober.
Thirteen Yank publishers turned down *Under the Volcano*,
On which he had laboured eight full years.
There then was Malc, sodden with tequila and mescal,
Rotted with failure of every kind,
Sitting down to write a thirty-one page letter
To J. Cape Esq., in Bedford Square, London,
Whose advisers were as myopic as the Yanks.
In Cuernavaca he showed me a draft of that letter—
Imagine having to defend a masterpiece!
I still remember a few of Malc's phrases:
It's hot music, a poem, a song, a tragedy, a comedy, a farce ...
It's a prophecy, a political warning, a cryptogram ...
The fascination of the different levels.
And yes, my friend, it was a novel too
That shafted deeply into mystery and myth.
Old Dante would have understood ...
Nel mezzo del cammin di nostra vita
In the middle of the road of our life
I came to myself in a dark wood
Where the straight way was lost ...
DON'T TALK TO ME OF BLOODY PUBLISHERS!'

CAPTAIN FOX'S DREAM

'Do you remember your dreams?' I asked.

'Rarely—but there's one I can't forget.
There was a butterfly in this dream,
Just an ordinary yellow powdery butterfly.
I caught it in my hand and it fluttered out
To circle half-heartedly.
I caught it again and squeezed harder.
I killed the butterfly
And watched a big drop of blood ooze out.
I thought: *It isn't squashed. I'll sell it.*
But the pet shop lady said:
"We don't buy butterflies".
I picked it up from the counter
And walked out with it.
I felt as dead as the butterfly'.

Fox paused and then he said:
'No prizes for interpretations'.

EZRA POUND IN OLD AGE

Beset by cataracts, crumpled by age
Yet he went to Delphi with Olga,
Stood at Joyce's grave in Zürich,
Returned briefly to God's own country,
Saw Marianne Moore there, Mary Hemingway,
But not his birthplace in Hailey, Idaho,
Was snubbed by Yevtushenko in Spoleto,
Flew to London for Eliot's memorial service
('Who is there now to share a joke with?')

'Where are you living?' a reporter asked.
'In hell', he answered simply,
Muttering with hand on heart, 'Here, here'.
Old Possum dead, William Carlos Williams gone,
The scythe dangling from every lamp-post,
Vanity's green tree rust-brown in the desert,
Guilt hollering through a ten-year silence
('Everything that I touch, I spoil'.)
And O the vast tiredness at eighty-seven,
The need to voyage home to Ithaca!

JAMES JOYCE

Now we recall that bitter, dogged Dubliner, James Joyce,
Whose yeasty chaos travelled Europe in his aching brain.
Trieste, Zürich, Paris, Rome and other cities
Knew this young exile buoyed on anger and contempt
For all that was provincial, meanly self-sufficing.
A furnace blazed in his mind's core perpetually
And would not give him rest from constant labour
Until the multi-imaged soul cascaded many thousand words
Barbed and pristine with a febrile, love-hate energy.
Silence, exile, cunning—these sharp keys he cut
To unlock the obdurate gate to Europe,
These keys made in his Dublin prison in friend-wasted days
When Ibsen, Jonson, Hauptmann floodlit each chamber
of his mind
And he determined not to honour those fierce claims
Of country, family and church: *I will not serve.*
Then think of him, half-blind and penniless in European towns
Racked by the restive *daemon* of creativeness,
Showing a will inflexible against the little streets
With hatred in their piping, rabble voices,
He ceaselessly dredging an oceanic mind for images
To haunt our splintered century and show us to ourselves,
Crying aloud with all the anguish of our time.

A ROOM

The light is central to this room:
Deep orange shade masking the bulb
And flinging shadows on the wall.
Aristide Bruant glances away from me,
Arrogant, cold master of cabaret
Pinned like an insect by Toulouse-Lautrec.
Across the rooftops rises the geometry
Of TV antennae, the window squares
Yellowing the night, signalling warmth
A dark-bright city cannot yield.
The eager clock hurries relentlessly
Below the Buddha on his gilded mount:
No questioning the circle of *his* calm
Nor that of Sherap, stocky Tibetan monk,
Whose hand these lines and circle drew
To beat the worldly devils off.
Two sketches on the wall behind my chair:
A German woman, dark, grave-eyed
With cryptic Mona Lisa look;
A heavy-faced young unsmiling man
Dreaming a long-forgotten dream,
This writer's buried yet unburied self.
An emptying glass at my right hand
On red-and-green checked tablecloth
That tells the countries of my heart,
While on the left an open book of poems
Begs for a final loving glance.
I close the book, refill the glass
Switch on a total stranger's voice.

A SUMMER DAY

Dream of a summer day: a hearse,
Bleached tombstones, gold letters glinting.
A stone forest in a city suburb:
Beloved husband; much-loved son;
Thy will, O lord, not ours be done.
Mother in the oak coffin; yes, at last
After much pain and long, hard years
That came to nearly eighty-eight.
Voiceless I stand, her often wayward boy,
While the minister intones grave words
I hear but don't quite grasp:
'Receive Elizabeth, Thy servant here'.
Sweetest of names, Elizabeth,
Each syllable a childhood bell.
Dismay and guilt in this neat wilderness,
I don't know where to turn my head.
Down, down, down. Wood unto earth.
Gravediggers tipped. All smoothly done.
Back now to the shining city
And the Victorians round the City Hall
Frozen forever in their sooty marble.
Gone, gone, gone. All gone
Back from the rectangles of the quiet dead.
Back to memory and guilt. Back to dismay.
Back to the nightmare of a summer day.

A CHILDHOOD MEMORY

Father in his swivel chair
Making a sudden intoxicated turn
Reek of whisky on his breath
Obscenities on his tongue.

Saturday night raw and damp
Figures shuffling past in pairs
Sunday chequered with psalms and hymns
After homework up the linoleumed stairs.

Monday blue-pocked with gusty cold
Haste to beat the bell at school
Neurotic clang and grind of trams
Life's earnest, no time to fool.

Initials carved on inky desk
Dreams of sirens, technicoloured seas
Palm trees awave in Eastern sunset
Bumpy ride home to sour realities.

DERRY

As a child in Derry I heard the shots
And the crackle of burning timber
That signalled the ancient quarrel
Of Prod and Papist, that ritual feud
Lingering on in a lost province
Where memories of long-ago battles
Are as fresh as today's headlines.
Memories of Siege and horror, of Lundy,
The Apprentice Boys and the Boom
And God-knows what fag-ends of history
Make a stirring tale for children
But light the fuse in the bitter heart.
Tales of blood and sectarian thunder
Lead to a coarse and brutal logic
Where my side is whiter than white
And yours black as a crow's wing.
Once more the thick urgent cries,
The pool of blood in the doorway,
The searing blaze of hate.

Yet I who have gone away
To safe and easy exile
Cannot just write them off
As simply ignorant thugs.

I, too, am involved in their crimes.

WORDS

If I were even half a mathematician I'd reckon up
How many words I've written or four-finger typed
In thirty-five years of feverish word-mongering
With hardly a day free of the White Goddess
Riding my back, her nails clawing my cheeks,
And the whore's tongue going nag, nag, nag;
Having shaken off the bitch for an hour
I must hurry from redder lips and sweeter nipples
Away home to sweat over the old Remington Portable,
Transmuting even Eros into words, words, words.
How count the active or passive voices, the solid nouns,
The sly adjectives describing their way into the act,
The adverbs brightly, crazily etc., the bastardly gerunds
Whose capering and grinning set my teeth on edge.
Oh, how I've wanted to strangle that White Lady!
Oh, this compulsion to make marks on paper when awake
Or, asleep, to swim in a gulf streaming with words
And after sleep to feel the tidal lift and fall
Of phrase and paragraph, sentence and stanza,
To hear the anxious cry of stop and semi-colon!

But one day, God knows, I'll take to brush and paint instead,
I'll show the hag who wears the trousers.
And, totally bananas, thinking I'm Dali or Picasso,
I shall make love to a piece of canvas or a blank wall.
I'll grow a long red beard that's utterly absurd
And I'll never, never, *never* write another word!

THE TRAVELLER

Norton Fitzwarren, Shepton Mallet,
Sheepwash, Black Torrington:*
Some such West-country place,
The time a century ago.

An evening black as tar
A knife of wind ice-edged
And never a star to bless the traveller
Nor even cur to argue with snap and bark.
A stranger rode up to the 'Fox and Hounds'.

Inside the oil lamps spluttered
Poured light in saffron pools
Polished the golden cider.
The traveller called for brandy,
The locals stared, froze into a hush
And crowded round the fire.

No one remembered later how it happened:
A callow youth guffawed, perhaps, to see
A gentleman join the rustic company
Or someone trod upon the stranger's foot
Or spoke a dialect word translated into insult
In the stranger's cold brain.

Putting down his glass he pulled a snake
Out of a pocket underneath his cloak.
'Apologise or die of snakebite', he rasped.
The landlord and the villagers stood agape
Like tableau figures made of wax.
A minute later all had fled
Except for the jelly-bellied landlord.
'Truly I'm sorry, sir', he puffed.

The traveller calmly ordered mutton chops,
Drank two quarts of ale and went to bed.

Hours later, Jack, an old labourer, died
Of a heart attack brought on by fright.
Young George stayed in bed for a whole week,
Others screamed in their anguished sleep
So that doctor and parson were hard pressed,
Prescribing and praying for weeks on end.
The greybeards met in council and declared:
' 'Twas the devil in disguise or we be Dutch'.

Then the landlord had a new sign painted,
Renamed his inn 'The Snake and Traveller'
Not far from Norton Fitzwarren, Shepton Mallet,
Sheepwash, Black Torrington,
Or some such Westward place.

CURSE

Son of a Scots manse though you were
I've taken the rare scunner against you,
You who thieve the golden hours of bairns,
You who bitch up the world's peoples
With dream-like images, coal-black lies,
You who have ended civilised conversation
And dished out licences to print banknotes,
May your soul shrink to the size of a midge
And never rest in a couthie kirkyaird*
But flicker across a million wee screens
And be harassed by T.V. jingles for ever and ever,
For thine's the kingdom of the *Televisor*,
You damnable bloody genius, John Logie Baird!*

A POET DYING

*in memory of Clifford Dyment**

Curtains draped against the noon heat,
A newspaper unopened whose tense headlines
Cry death in this blind room.

Sleep that brings the green dreams back:
A dappled *As You Like It* forest
Ardent with Dukes, Fools, Rosalinds.

Then slag-heaps, railway cuttings, stunted trees,
Telegraph poles, metallic bird-like artefacts,
Pit-heads: the furniture of his unloved Midlands.

Boyhood trains to London and the sleek South
Trains to the West racing to Monmouthshire,
Roman and Arthurian Caerleon, legends in the heart

That fade to film of dew on evening hillfield,
Gunshot splitting the sky, resonance of collie bark,
Welsh cousins' voices singsonging to heaven.

An eyeless stranger blacking the horizon,
A ripped coat upon a leafless bush,
The sunset furnace burning turning burning.

from

A BRIGHT MASK:
NEW & SELECTED POEMS
(1985)

REVISITING BELFAST

Revisiting Belfast I recall most vividly
The startling red of the trams of childhood—
No red will ever be so red again—
And the torn posters, half-hinged on hoardings,
Behind which we played our hide-and-seek
Till the grey-lead dusk had called us home
After the realities in practice's sharp school.
The very air was different then
(Since I was different then).
Childhood preferred the artistic vision,
Vision without performance, without satiety,
Transmuting the stones to all rare minerals.
The air was brittle then, like glass
You saw through; that kindly was opaque to one's own skeleton.
I remember at school the trouble with masters
Frowning: cutting the key to fit the normal lock.
But stirring ashes kindles no fire
And one isn't yet sufficiently old
To lament the quick change of Act—
There is only another scene.
Belfast is a film of rapid memories—
Loitering homewards from school, discussing heroes
Or cycling for adventure past scarlet traffic lights
Or mitching to Bellevue to view the smoke-tossed lough.
And then the first whisper of desire,
The shamefaced, timid overture,
The quick rebuff—and sawdust in the mouth.
I think of those forgotten seaside trips
We called excitement: the liquid sand,
Caves to explore, tall cliffs to strut on
Far from industrial fog and fug.
But, most vividly of all,
I see the barbarous, shrieking red
Of Belfast's trams of childhood.

FATHER AND SON

I can't remember how it happened,
How hatred seeded and grew rank,
A tall weed that dwarfed us both
And flourished till it stank.

Yet that isn't the whole story.
I remember evenings when, father and son,
We walked the velvety spring streets
And greeted the blossoms one by one.

Images become blurred, then clear
To harshness, violence; but still
Behind the bitter word, the angry gesture,
I find the love that neither wished to kill.

Rest in peace, my father, trespass forgiven,
The dark stains whitened out. Today
The siren screams our armistice,
The angry dwarfs ride fast away.

AUDEN

His armoured presence filled the youthful sky,
Dawn Viking of the Utopian longship,
Doctor's son who x-rayed sick Europe.
Technologist of emotions, flippant teacher,
Lost leader, crossword puzzler, Anglican Prospero,
Lover of limestone landscape and opera,
His ageing face mapped out an era's neurosis.
The gods smiled on his swift coming and going.
Wordman Extraordinary, find in Valhalla
The Great Good Place of *skald** and hero.

OLD ZECHARIAH*

His beard a dark forest flecked with white,
His face scored with wrong turnings,
Old Zechariah shuffles at the altar
In robes threadbare and rumpled.
Ah, how the children mock him,
Call out in the streets 'Old spindleshanks!'
They know he trades in daft visions
And Elizabeth has been barren for his sins.

But now he peers out of red-rimmed eyes.
'What's that I hear? A son?
Born to Elizabeth? To be named John?
To be a herald? Filled with the Holy Spirit?
To bring back Israel to the Lord, our God?
Never to know the taste of wine?
Mockery! Mockery! Mockery!
This devil claims the name of Gabriel'.

The priest falls dumb until the day
They come to circumcise the child.
Suddenly the old man's lips and tongue
Unfreeze and utter their eager prophecy.
The thin shanks dance as at his wedding feast
And Zechariah's words ring silver-clear—
John, John, John, John—among the Judaean hills.

A MAN CALLED SIMEON*

The prices were high in Jerusalem,
Twenty shekels for a pair of turtle doves,
So the young people paid through the nose
For the offering the Law required.
The temple was noisy, none too clean.
Some testy Jews gestured in fury
And looked as if they might come to blows.
A centurion walked past, his sword imperial.
It was not at all what they expected
After a tiresome journey from the village,
The threats of bandits and beggars.
But they were not the sort to complain,
The woman in blue and her mild husband.
A man came up and said he was Simeon.
He must have been eighty if a day
Despite his great white quiff.
They were surprised and not surprised,
It just seemed so right, so natural,
And they let him hold the child.

'At last, at last to hold Him in my arms.
His light will shine among the nations,
The glory of our people, Israel'.

Even the centurion had stopped to listen
And so had a knot of moneylenders.

Then Simeon peered into the mother's face:
'Mary, you will be hurt most bitterly'.
She took the baby back from him,
Her eyes alive with love and fear.
'My son', she said, 'My dear, dear son'.

CAPTAIN FOX'S CHILDHOOD
HOLIDAY IN IRELAND

Clouds dangerously low overhead.
Narrow fields imprisoned by stone walls.
Black clockwork figures in braces,
Felling the innocent tall corn.
Decrepit villages idling in the sun.
Jack-frosted windows in the pubs
That sported names like KELLY.
The tangle of mid-summer roads.
The dusty honeysuckled hedges.
A dead rabbit rusty and flat.
The wreck of abandoned homesteads.
The tribal north astir with drums.
Brogues thickening as father soldiered south,
Sergeant-majoring, joking, blustering
When he gargled his black beer—
Rebels? I'd shoot the fuckin' lot.
Then a cottage by the chattering sea:
Low ceilings; worm-eaten rafters;
An oil lamp's angry splutter;
A Protestant Bible with a metal clasp;
Edge-curled photos of khaki lads
Killed at Somme and Dardanelles;
The windblown stench from a manure heap;
The intoxication of a rose garden;
The rub and rustle of mother's silk;
A fortnight's holiday millennia long.

THE PHOTOGRAPHER

Klein, the photographer, was playing tennis.
Called away to answer the phone
In a nearby café—the *locale* was Paris.

Light-footed, pleased with himself,
He had volleyed to his friends' applause.
Now a brush with reality.

A mirror showed a wodge* of ageing flesh,
Anxiety cracking a bright mask,
Eyes two abandoned islands.

Feeling like a million dollars
A bent dime glared back at him.
Mirrors, unlike cameras, never lie.

ENJAMBEMENT

'I see words broken into the next line—
I suppose there is a technical term for it'.
So writes a friend about someone else's poem.

Now I think of the word *enjambement*.
I am fifteen again, crazed by girls,
Bullied by the vowels of Mr. McAdam.

Mr. McAdam drilled us in French proprieties,
Spat out his learning in a Belfast accent thick
As the boys' lips stumbling over *avoir* and *être*.

He cuffed me once or twice, shouted abuse
For my abuse of the French language.
(He also warned me against D.H. Lawrence.)

Later I learned he had dropped dead
But I didn't feel sorrow or pleasure.
Now I think of the word *enjambement*.

TIN FLOWERS

The old Mexican woman
Hobbles in the street:
'Tin flowers for graves,
Pretty, best quality.
Flores para los muertos,
Coronas para los muertos'.

Their brilliance shatters my eyes.
Hepatitis, cancer, malaria, syphilis,
Come take your pick, good sirs,
Red, blue, yellow, green.

'Beautiful flowers, pure tin flowers,
I shall not rob you,
Colours of the rainbow,
Buy Maria's flowers'.

I empty my trouser pockets
Throw my loose change at her,
And she grins and grins,
Bows to the generous señor
Opens the cavern of her mouth
To pour out a hoarse aria:
'Flores para los muertos,
Coronas para los muertos'.

from

CARNIVAL AT THE RIVER

(1990)

CARNIVAL AT THE RIVER

The procession of ghosts shuffles by,
Faceless, bannerless, blobs in a landscape
Of dead trees, rotted flowers.
Gradually the blobs dissolve into people.
Father steps out in Edwardian style,
Links arms with mother in her flowered hat.
There's cousin Jim, his gun lusting for snipe.
Aunt Tillie's fox fur dangles at her neck.
Teachers pace by in funereal gowns.
Boys in uniform, bare-kneed, sulk past
As if they'd been cheated of a holiday.
Stewart pushes a 1930s Raleigh bike,
Willie McIlwaine drools over an oval ball.
I turn on my side and hope for easy sleep
Away from the images of childhood
But the procession sidles into dream.
I am walking beside grandfather.
He plucks his beard, tells me softly:
'We're going to the carnival.
We are gathering at the river'.
I feel cold, my guts tighten.
Father's father, take my arm!
Grandfather holds me, quotes Beckett:
'Je n'ai rien contre les cimetières'.
We laugh, walk arm-in-arm to the carnival,
The gathering at the river.

ST. ANDREW'S DAY, 1985

St. Andrew's Day, blind November fumbling
The hurt leaves, bleached gutter orphans.
Half-light domesticates raw brick.
A mediocre day, not to be remembered.
It's 2 p.m. at Ladbroke Grove. I board a bus.
The mourners are gathering at Glengarriff.
Is it drizzling there? I hear the rain
Touch-typing an elegy on the bay waters.
Though in her will she said 'No flowers'
Our daughter will place veronica on the coffin
Borne through the woods to the old Killeen.
Will the funeral go to plan, discreetly,
Even in the drizzle I imagine falling
On the lands of Gael and Planter?
I say a London goodbye to a lost wife,
Remember our time of roses, promises,
The silvered sea at Ardnagashel,
Earrings of fuchsia in the hedgerows,
Hope arching, like a rainbow, over all.

FATHER

Gaunt face, brush moustache,
Dark hair, lean frame.
I, a sandy, Nordic child
Took him for Spanish.
I was my mother's son,
He wasn't our tribe.
I'd wait outside the 'Britannia'
Then lead him home,
A tear on my cheek.
I remember his tantrums,
Red-rimmed eyes on fire,
Thick whiskey voice.
Once, pushed too far,
I reached for a hatchet,
Won my long trousers.
Yet there were moments—
Vivid with gestures—
When I sat on his knee,
Gently combed his hair.

UNCLE GEORGE

Sometimes he'd grip my hand
In his rough bulbous gentle fist,
Then guide me over fence and *sheugh*.*
I'd watch him out of big child eyes
Half hope to see the beast run free.
I'd hear the whole townland explode,
The chuckle at his hunter's skill.
Guns, harrows, ploughs, his holy artefacts,
His pulpit was his workshop,
Toil his route to paradise.
Sunday saw him dressed in navy serge,
Edwardian cut as in his youth,
Knife creases made by mattress weight.
In Bible mood he'd hold his peace
Huddle close to the turf fire
Wrestle with John Knox's God.
He prophesied I'd live to see
The sun turn black at noon,
Earthquakes, meadows red with blood.
Each March 1 call to mind
His orchard massed with daffodils,
Their dance of life, their dance of death.

UNCLE JACK

Mother's wedding photo shows him quite the swell,
Hair middle-parted, white waistcoat, buttonhole,
His three sisters' golden boy.
Then letters stopped; we wondered why

He didn't turn up for his mother's funeral.
At sixteen I leapt the Irish Sea,
Tracked him to his shop in Birmingham,
Found him thick-waisted, slicing bacon.

One Sunday he drove his Morris
Into Worcestershire, picture-postcard England
Of half-timbered inns, oak leaves,
A world away from dole queues, idle cranes.

Once on his Edgbaston lawn we stood
Uncle and nephew, he jovial in a thunderstorm,
I with trembling knees.
He showed me his Freemason apron, jewels,

A certificate on imitation parchment
That proved him a Mark Mason,
Master of dotty ceremony, mumbo-jumbo.
He said it was for charity, no use in business.

I admired his semi-detached, its velvety moquette*—
French polishing, Axminster carpets*—
Longed to affect such style myself.
In the city centre I bought a *Daily Worker*,

Held a teetotal wake for Spain's Republic.
I took home news of Uncle Jack's prosperity,
The Derry orphan God had smiled on—
The work ethic in working order.

Years on, the *Luftwaffe* wrecked his shop,
Brought on a fatal heart attack.
I've got the jewels and Masonic apron—
No longer lust after moquette, Axminster carpets.

PHOTOGRAPH

for my daughter Arethusa

I've leafed through my blue album
And found that photo you spoke of.
Date's on the back—December '47—
In the green ink I then affected.
I shudder at that long winter
You arrived at the Rotunda
Shocking me into fatherhood.
In the photo you are an owlish
Ten-month old, high in your chair,
Eyes like black cherries
Darting at the photo-flash.
Your mother's on the left,
Elegant in her white bow.
I'm on the right—smiling.

COUSIN WILLIE

A country boy, he came to town
But found no job to fit his style.
His talent was for guns and uniforms,
Shoes burnished like patent leather,
Shirts like laundered snow.
He marched to the drum of authority
Whistled the tribal tune.
Once he called me 'Bolshevik',
I shot him with a glance.
Our islands had no bridge,
No Gulf Stream warmed our lands.
Impatient for the coming war,
He joined the Brylcreem boys.
I watched his train steam off.
His farewell act a mock salute,
I clenched an unraised fist.

INSTEAD OF FLOWERS

Granny McCrea, plump-faced, brooched,
Every inch eminently Victorian
Cased in black from head to foot,
Long widowed, victim of a bent solicitor,
Loved me, her only grandchild,
Yet used the tawse* to drive the devil out.
She bossed her daughters, gave son John
To the grocer's trade in Birmingham,
Worked until the night she died.
I was her dream: a doctor's brass plate
Or, better still, a pulpit and Geneva gown.
Outside her room the rasp of trams,
Red monsters bound for urgent destinations.
Inside, the gas mantle's cosy hum,
The yellow light by which she read
The Christian Herald, C.H. Spurgeon's sermons.
Bronchitis killed her when I was ten.
The motor hearse drove westward to Tyrone:
Leckpatrick and her husband David's grave.
I cried and cried and cried.
She bequeathed me a purse of sovereigns;
A cracked brown photo; a conscience.

BAD BOOKS

Bad books could raise the Devil—
A man he knew had done just that
And later hanged himself.
The story came from Uncle George
Who, neighbours said, had never lied.
Impressed, I vowed to spurn bad books,
To sip the master spirits' blood,
Read all Shakespeare by twenty-one,
In time grow wise, armoured in light.
Yet bad books sidled on to my shelves—
Lightweight novels, shallow philosophy
That dared to join the Great and Good.
But who can tell what's bad, what's good?

SUNDAY IN COUNTY MONAGHAN, 1935

Dewy rose-bud in buttonhole
Hair slicked, violet-scented.
The minister prays for farmers' weather.
The harmonium swells in reedy praise.
I daydream beside still waters.
Outside the crumbling church they gather,
A dwindling clan, greying:
Adairs, Gillespies, Wilsons, Smyths—
King's men without a King.
Chat of government and crops,
Taxes, swine fever, price of land,
Sons prospering 'across the water'.
A drive back over powdery roads
And up the hunchback lane to chicken,
Uncle George's talk of Armageddon
And why the Kaiser lost the war.
A stroll across the townland.
Brontë pages skimmed under the elm,
Tea in Belleek china, ginger snaps,
'Throw Out the Lifeline' baritoned
On the wind-up gramophone.
A spin on the gleaming sports bike
A burnt-out house, thatched cottages,
'Up Dev!' chalked on a wall.
'Brave day', cries Pat O'Byrne,
Jetting an arc of tobacco juice.
The twilit fields with cousin Jane,
A collie bark from Kelly's yard.

CITY

A swathe of mist muffles the firs.
The wind's a north-east lash.
Light by light indicts the dark.
Images dissolve, come sharp again.
Today some soldiers on patrol
Prised up my childhood—
Marches, gunfire in the streets,
Barriers to separate the tribes.
This city, heir to an historic spite,
Learns nothing, seldom forgets,
Honours the tart negative.
The room grown dark, rain drums,
The central heating doesn't work.
I'd better go to bed for warmth.
Perhaps I'll dream away the *angst*,
The slogans and tomorrow's dead.

PREACHER

On wings of hair
He soars to heaven.
He warns, exhorts,
Fights sin, the Devil,
Like Amos or Micah.
I suck an acid drop,
Stare at a window,
Watch a fly examine a bald head.
His thunder ceases,
Hawk turns into dove.
He leans over the pulpit,
Confides the Devil is a loser.
I suck another acid drop.

CHURCH AND COVENANT

The kitschy* statues bleed.
This theatre of God
Acts out a Latin poetry
A heretic can't translate.
I think of pitch pine pews
A northern childhood knew.
I wrestled with John Knox
Who ghostly in the aisles
Whispered 'Thou Shalt Not'.
I think of ancestors who lived
For Kirk and Covenant.
They feared the anti-Christ,
The Roman Man of Sin,
Scorned English mitres too.
Aware of thumbscrew, rack,
They chose a martyr's stance.
I lack their bigot pride,
Their certainty of Truth.
I chose a slacker way,
An anxious tolerance.

JOHN HEWITT

Sports jacket, corduroys, red tie.
A voice in Belfast middle-class
Proclaims the Marxist line of '38.
A plump young man, moustached,
Defines the issue of the time.

'Some want conscription'—pause—
'But others are of military age'.
'Who's that?' I ask. Boyd whispers:
'Another John— surname's Hewitt'.

I'll pass him on Stranmillis Road.
'Hello', he'll say, abrupt and shy,
Museum man not yet in Coventry.
One day he bids me call him John,
Asks me to his Mount Charles flat.
He's not a man who seeks
Confessions, drunk alliances,
The praise of coteries,
Lounge bar politics.

We rarely write or phone
To bridge the Irish Sea.
He and McFadden tried to break
The mould of bigotry.
Last met in '84, John bearded,
Frail, eye-troubled, stick in hand,
Snug in the *Châlet d'Or*.
We chat of friends, our craft,
The temper of the local streets.

Talk done, I watch him walk away,
Admire his stubborn gait.

COMRADE TED

*for Thomas McCarthy**

Hunger, illegal work, being anonymous:
The shoulders of Charles Edward Fox support
These pillars of the V.I. Lenin Church.
The Captain's son and heir, he would uproot
His father's spreading laurel tree
That sheltered such as Yeats the Senator,
Laureate of custom and of ceremony.
Instead he's set a bitter plant,
The Ragged Robin of the common field.
Victory to the workers! Action now!

I've heard he lives at Shepherd's Bush
Without a mistress, wife or child,
In shabby rooms, spartan and chill
Like those he knew at Royal Gordonstoun.
Posters, memos, pamphlets of dissent,
Minutes of committees poised for strikes,
Tape recorders, jostle in his living room.
The postman brings a sack of mail each day.
Charles Edward, like his father, travels light,
Wings swift on urgent errands too.
Sometimes he goes to preach the Word
In driving voice, now somewhat hoarse,
That rasps out tags from Lenin, Trotsky, Marx.
A pulpit man who intrigues if needs must,
A grass-green incorruptible who hammers those
Who dare to stray from true parameters,
To many known as Honest Comrade Ted.

I wrote to ask for filial help
In research for the Captain Fox biography
And six weeks later got the terse reply:
'All father's files and letters burnt'.
A ruthless father and a ruthless son.
But I shall be avenged, my friend,
For if God grant me years enough
I swear to ferret out the secrets of Ted Fox.
Record, discuss, footnote, assess,
Press-ganging Freud and Adler for the task
I'll trace each action with a pedant's lust
And write two *Lives* instead of one.

ONE MUST GO

They come in threes but one must go.
Pig, cow, hen: one must go.
Forest, tree, table; up, down, and.
One must go. Sea, beer, sand;
Herring, cod, whale; coffee, vodka, tea;
Yeats, Auden, Shaw; Thames, Lomond, Lee;
Life, death, breath; cat, dog, canary;
Apple, carrot, pear; queen, ghost, fairy.
Five, four, three; who, but, which;
Shoe, sandal, boot; poor, wise, rich.
Quick, pretty, slow; one must go.
They come in threes but one must go.

from

NEW & UNCOLLECTED
POEMS

(c. 1995)

KINSKY

What's become of Kinsky since he flew to Ankara?
He said he went to contact Kurdish friends.
Months later, a postcard dropped into my hall:
'Great is Diana of the Ephesians, Greetings. *K.*'

Rumours abound: brain-box of a Kurdish cell,
Torture by the Turks, assassination, suicide,
Arms smuggler doing a brisk business, a double agent.
Others say he is writing a novel in Hebrew.

According to his own account—
Half-Jew, half-Kurdish, born in Amsterdam,
Trained in linguistics, a Polytechnic tutor.
I remember Kinsky's hooded eyes,
A ghetto child squinting at daylight.

A week before his flight he and I lunched
With Carrington-Smythe at the Athenaeum,
Heard how our Foreign Office friend
Mislaid some papers, nearly caused a minor war.
Carrington-Smythe boomed into creamy laughter
That spoke of grouse moors, manor houses,
Tennis on an ample Suffolk lawn.

Kinsky didn't quite understand,
His English too correct, too literal.
Later he dropped his bomb.
'In a metal box in the fridge', he said,
'I keep my mother's ashes'.
We thought it his counter-joke
But no, the man was serious.

I wonder what's become of Kinsky*
Since he gave us all the slip.

HOMECOMINGS

I stared with brown eyes
Down to the Foyle waters,
Held out a hand with sugar
To a breadcart horse.
Et ego in Arcadia ...
Among Derry oaks St. Colum
'numbered the stars of heaven
this teacher of all things
this Dove, this Colum Cille'.

City of Walls
City of Siege
Jewel of the north
Maiden of the west
Undone by drums and cymbals
Fat rats! Fat rats!
Fed on the Irish dead
Fat rats!
One for a shillin'

A stranger among strangers
I look for my house of birth.
Pulled down years ago
I show the paper: 'I certify ...'
Ich bin ein Derryman
A stranger grips my hand.

I dawdle at the Guildhall,
Buy postcards, a newspaper,
Watch armoured cars
Patrolling history.
Over a Chinese sweet-and-sour
I chat to a local.
He files the claws
Of tribal words
For walls have ears.

The March wind
Body-searches the daffodils
I sip tea in a café
Read the despatches
Of bombing, kidnap—
'Teach us to care
and not to care'.

Donemana in Tyrone—
Grandmother's parish
Of Smyths and sheep.
Dour stone walls
Divide, eavesdrop
In a scrubbed landscape.
Home at last
To wet and winds.

GOALS

A street singer is droning:
'You are all I have, sonny boy'.
Al Jolson reigns OK.
Corner boys scuffle like sparrows
As they pitch and toss for pennies.
Cigarette smoke blues the twilight
Eddies off to the shipyard.
A boy, messenger of the gods,
Lithe Mercury in uniform,
Dashes past on a red bicycle,
Telegram in his pouch,
Drama in a dozen words.

I clasp a football reeking of leather.
I'm captain, Willie's centre-forward,
Our jackets mark the goalposts.
We scramble over cobbles, graze knees,
Get shouted at by a housewife
Anxious for her glossy windows.
The lamplighter with his pole
Startles the mantles into life,
Gaslight signals our end-game.
The ball bounces towards a magnetic field,
Goal on dream goal
And the victor's wreath
Lures us to great Saturdays,
Thunder on the terraces.

ON THE LANDING

I was sure he crouched on the landing
That one night he would puff my candle out
That my legs would give way
That he would laugh darkly
That he would carry me off
In a sack on his back.
Night after night I dilly-dallied,
Invented excuses, moped,
Doodled on blotting paper
Upset bottles of ink
Begged for mugs of buttermilk.
At last, sentenced to bed,
I loitered on the stairs
Stared at the yellow flame
Both sword and shield.
Then, desperate, reckless,
I shut my eyes
Ran as if Old Nick himself
Were on my heels.
Secure in the attic
I prayed as I'd been taught
Yet only sleep could banish
The creature of the landing.

AT THE GARRICK CLUB

Old pals, we supped on oysters, venison,
Let a scarlet ribbon of *Château de l'Amour*,
Hinting at raspberries, ease down our throats.
'It sure yanks my chain', remarked a Chicagoan.
In a Club ghosted by Garrick, Mrs. Pat,*
We guzzled, sprawled, toasted Captain Fox
While Carrington-Smythe of the F. O. rambled,
Did the Grand Tour from Calais to the Caucasus.
He spoke of Captain Fox's exploits in Cairo
Of how our hero played the Lawrence card,
Mastered the camel, had contacts in the *souk*,*
Did business in demotic Arabic.
Ah Fox, old boy, suave actor-manager
Who took the world for stage, your friends
Erect a pyramid of memories.
Heavily night-capped I fumbled out
Into the jungle of the lighted dark.
Then, on the National Gallery steps
Flanked by junkies, yobs, drop-outs,
I nodded to a drunk Lord Nelson.
'My love to Emma', I cried out.
Like Fox, he knew the bloody score.

THE ONLY EMPEROR

A wreath of mist circles the sky
A swirl of leaves veined ruby-red
A brisk north chill confers
An October welcome on an October child.
At the station passengers
Huddle for buses to the City Hall
Delayed, so rumour goes, by terrorists.
Impatient, I begin to walk,
Adrenalin on quick demand.
There's an area ribboned off:
Soldiers, ambulancemen stand-to
Impassive, heavy with authority.
I hear a bomb explode
Smoke gushes from a roof.
I walk, intent on Wallace Stevens
Of the *Hartford Accident & Indemnity Corporation*.
A policeman answers softly:
'Yes, you can go up Ann Street,
Cross here, go through the subway'.
On this October day, an October child
Now drifting into age
Dark-suited, briefcase under arm,
Sees workmen, students, circulate
Bent on ephemeral business.
Still brooding on Wallace Stevens,
Words echo in my head
His ambiguity my ambiguity
On this October day of mist and mystery
When I know, as Wallace Stevens knew,
The only emperor is the emperor of ice cream.*

THE NEW COMMANDMENTS

1st. No other God exists than Mighty Me.
2nd. Worship the vulgar idols of T.V.
3rd. Say 'God' when laughing or to be provoking.
4th. No Sunday overtime? You must be joking!
5th. Revile your Dad, break Mother's heart.
6th. Remember murder is a necessary art.
7th. Adultery clearly shows sophistication
8th. And theft's the hallmark of a clever nation.
9th. False witness leads to increased dividends
10th. And envy's the prerogative of friends.

JERUSALEM

'In Finland I felt I had lost my God',
Said the Lutheran Finn in Jerusalem,
'But now God speaks to me in Finnish
His voice thundering in my ears,
The grammar, the idiom perfect.
Praise Him! Praise Him!'
A kilted Wee Free* from Stornoway
Rides a white donkey through the Old City,
Intones a metrical psalm:
The Lord's my shepherd, I'll not want,
    He makes me down to lie
In pastures green: he leadeth me
    The quiet waters by.
There's a Jewish boy from Finchley
Who flexes his muscles, calls himself Samson,
Carries a poster cursing Philistines,
Is sometimes dragged screaming from pillars.
Others declare themselves the Christ, the Messiah,
A man hanged himself for being Judas.
Christian, Jew, Moslem, anyone can go down
With Jerusalem fever—syndrome, if you insist.
An aeon ago as a child I sang
Of Jerusalem awash with milk and honey,
A city of old under the fathering sun,
Daybreak to nightfall, its hymn
Pure as water, holy as prayer
Without end, without beginning.

KAVANAGH IN BALLSBRIDGE*

A poet in Raglan Road, No. 19,
Slammed Yeats with words obscene.

In Donegal tweeds and crumpled hat
He'd bellow greetings, seldom chat.

Mention such as Austin Clarke
He would splutter, hoarsely bark:

'Bloody ould bags
Not worth twenty fuckin' fags'.

At any time of night or day
Half Ballsbridge could hear him say:

'Auden puts them all to flight—
The others are a load of shite'.

Nobel Yeats then dead and gone
Kavanagh would carry on.

Lost his love one autumn time
Poured his anguish into rhyme

Made a song of loveliness
From a welling of distress

When dark Hilda ran away
At the dawning of the day.

AUNT TILLIE

When mother went away
You took her place.
You showed me how
To pull my socks on
Master the alphabet
Spell words like 'icicle'.
You told me wonder tales—
Jack the Giant Killer,
The Three Bears.
You bandaged my cut knees
Bought me a Raleigh bike,
A Coventry thoroughbred,
Saw I was schooled
Took on my feckless Dad.
I veered from policies
That you endorsed
But kept your moral stance
As best I could.
I travel the road
Through the dead years
Back to your love.

OPENING THE DOOR

i.m. Beatrice Behan[*]

I knock, I knock.
I challenge the silence.
Knock! Knock! Knock!
I open the door into the room.
The blinds are drawn.
A bedside light is burning.
A glass of water stands on the table.
It's exactly 11.22 a.m.
She's in her bed, decently covered,
Her right hand outstretched,
A ring on her finger.
But she does not speak—
Ah, Beatrice was always the quiet one,
Walking her dogs Klaus and Karla
Beside the Dodder river,
Cycling home on the footpath
Noiselessly, with a Mona Lisa smile.
Upstairs I dial a number
While down in the street
People drift towards the Angelus
And across the way a honeyed wall
Is neutral under a March sky.

WATCHING

The masked man stared from a balcony
Named my name, said: 'We're watching you'.
My flesh stiffened into veined marble
Froze to a statue in a frock coat
An artefact for vandals, pigeons.

I dragged my weight to Sam's flat.
He glanced up from his word processor.
'I like your outfit', he grinned.
'Have you been time travelling?'
He massaged his brush moustache
Carelessly lit a cigarette.
'Watching is their business'.
Uncomforted, tears salted my eyes.
Sam smiled, grasped my hand.
'I must finish my story'.
I walked, a Victorian, to the City Hall.
Nobody bothered to notice my frock coat.
Until it started to pour, I hung around,
Then the yobs scarpered to doorways
Sober citizens crouched under brollies
Buses swished through a waterbed.

Suddenly the rain stopped and a rainbow
Caressed the dome of the City Hall.
I trudged off in my frock coat
Wondering if Sam had finished his story.

QUEEN OF THE BUCKET SHOP

*for Jack Midgley**

Eager war-maker, failed spy-catcher,
Trade Union basher, free speech smasher,
But oh how her enemies grow!—
Nurses and teachers, Anglican preachers,
Sour ex-Ministers glum in a row.
She grinds the pensioners and the poor,
Courts City slicker, Yuppie boor,
Kisses the mighty Yankee dollar.
Hear the Iron Lady holler:
Privatise, privatise!
I'm the only true Conserva*tive*.
I am Queen of the Bucket Shop,
My Tory reign will have no stop!'
Yet enemies and problems grow
And one fine day they'll make her go!

THE CALL

*for Jack W. Weaver**

I can state it plainly now:
It has not been what I expected.
Away back in my boyhood
I dreamed in the twilight,
Lost in a book,
And as the light faded
Heard a voice from a garden
Calling me softly
To a dew-drenched Eden.

I spent fresh mornings there,
An eager apprentice
Active in the sun.

In the null years
The garden grew rank.
I strayed from it
Into the mute forest
Of naked trees.

Yet the dream came back.
I returned to a garden of sorts,
Weeded, planted.
A few people visited.

Now in late autumn
There are flowers in bloom
Though the evenings are chill.
Yet I must repeat:
Things are not what I expected.

from

PROTESTANT
WITHOUT A HORSE

(1997)

AT BRENDAN BEHAN'S DESK

Full seven years I've sat
And scribbled at this desk:
Cards, letters, poems, autosnaps,
Diary entries, shopping lists,
While Beatrice down below hoarded
Memories of Brendan in a clutter
Of paintings, posters, photos,
With, for company, two dogs.

To Brendan's ghost I must confess
My orderly grey days.
At moments I'd like to be out
Emptying glasses in the pubs
Of Dublin town, blarneying
To actors, poets, drunks,
Then taxi-ing back to *Cuig**
Not earlier than three a.m.,
Rousing the solid citizens,
Telling an uncaring world
How 'that old triangle
Went jingle-jangle
Along the banks of the Royal Canal'.

Instead, I sit at Brendan's desk,
Reading, scribbling, drinking coffee—
A Protestant without a horse.

PROCESSION

based on the painting 'The Twelfth of July, Portadown' (1928)
by Sir John Lavery

A silken banner held aloft,
Three sashed horsemen,
One horse as laundered white
As the king's own steed,
Three Lambeg drummers thundering,
A flute player stepping ahead.

Behind, the ranked brethren of the Lodges,
The grey-blue houses roused from sleep,
The smudge that is the Union Jack.

The sons of William march today,
Recall the ancient feud,
Its sacred place names:
Derry, Aughrim, Enniskillen and the Boyne.

The past invades the present,
The present lives in the past,
The future will never come.

I.M. LESLIE OWEN BAXTER, 1919-1995

Above the crackle of our Philco Five
I listened to the scream from Nuremberg:
Ein Volk, Ein Reich, Ein Führer!
In Hitler's year of '33 I went to grammar school,
Proud in my uniform with its blue monogram,
Eager for Latin and the Rugby field.

First day I chanced upon a tall, shy boy
Who lugged around a case of books,
An earnest scholar but unlikely friend.

Friendship's bud exploded into flower
When in the locker room a boy who jostled him
Felt my clenched fist hard upon his nose.

We walked together through the cosy dusk
Years on, engrossed in dreams, anxieties,
The future stretching out in black or rose.

Since he has left me, the familiar streets
Stare back into a stranger's eye.
The city's foreign now, not his and mine.

The old and easy tag maintains
That time can heal the wound of loss.
Not so, not so, not so.

WALKING AWAY

Fifteen years together, then a curt goodbye
And a quickstep out to the heedless streets
From a marriage that must die.

Fifteen years of hope and doubt and tension—
How could he separate 'is', 'was', 'had been',
How could he unknot reality from self-deception?

Five years of sweetness and five of growing away,
Then five bethistled and weeded years
And a sky blacking the day.

Yet courage, he knew, must win in the end,
So he strode away with his head in the air,
Closing the chapter on 'Let's pretend'.

FINDING A CAT

A clever man said: 'There's no cat in that room'.
A clever woman said: 'The room's too dark to see a cat in'.
A child said: 'I heard a pussy miaowing'.

I thought: 'The child is right.
I'll go in and won't come out
Till I find that cat,
However dark the room,
Even if the cat is black'.

After a long time I came out,
Bloody from scratches,
Half-sorry I'd ever ventured in.
In my arms I carried a cat,
Vicious, black, beautiful.

FLYING INTO ATLANTA

A velvet evening at fall's end,
Day in retreat, I flying high
Look down on diamond lights.
John Keats, come with me now.
Let's travel in these realms
Un-misted, mellow, fruitful,
And drink from brimming beakers
Above this city's radiance,
Nor speak of hemlock, nightingales,
Or northern islands we have fled.
Through this rich Georgian sky
We'll ride in dazzlement
Deep in romantic images
Yet hear a voice proclaim:
O my America, my new-found land!

A NEW FLAT

I sit in a new flat, all new paint,
New desk, new chairs, new tables.
In the garden there are roses
Asleep in the mild October air.
There's a stone wall around the garden,
Now emerald after its summer ochre.
I can see a public call box,
Then over the road a Catholic church,
Joyce's *Stella Maris*, Star of the Sea,
Its green cone spearing heaven.

Hidden from view stands another church,
De-consecrated, where once Presbyterians
Came to sing psalms, hear sermons,
Before the Harp replaced the Crown.

I, no longer at Brendan Behan's desk,
But at my own (Irish cherry wood)
Take writing paper from a drawer
Scrawl my first letters from Sandymount.

This morning, waking, I cradled
A mouthful of words, seedlings
I hoped might flower into a poem.
Those words are vanished now,
Fallen into a limbo I can't reach.

Old Father Sun is working overtime,
His siren warmth sedates me.
I'll resist his call no longer:
'Come out and catch my gold,
Let poems wait for wind, for rain'.

from

CAPTAIN FOX: A LIFE

(2000)

OPERATION JUBILEE

Francais! Ceci est un coup de main et non pas l'invasion.[*]

Fox showed me a leaflet he had preserved
From a business appointment in Dieppe on 19th August, 1942,
When he'd been on a day trip with some Canadians.
They called it *Operation Jubilee.*

'I'll always remember a notice that read:
Chasse gardée. Entrée interdite sous peine de poursuite.[*]
A Canadian bully-boy riddled it with gunfire.
The raid? A shambles, yes, a total shambles
Lightened by the occasional ludicrous incident—
A Colonel surrendering with his men to a German captain.
Salutes from each and congratulations from the Colonel
On the efficiency of the Captain's troops.
Warriors from a fading tapestry
Heel clicking in a butcher's shop'.

'And then the beaches insulted with corpses,
The anarchic architecture of death and wreckage,
The screams, the hastily bandaged heads.
I'll spare the details you can see in Goya'.

'I went back there a while ago.
There's a stone of remembrance near the cemetery.
On which they've cut the words:
Their Name Liveth for Evermore'.

'Ah yes, as a Sergeant from Toronto put it—
Buddy, it was one helluva trip'.

LIFE WITHOUT THE CAPTAIN

Day's grey acreage, night's staring globes,
Bills, heavy colds, strikes, price rises,
Rotting stumps of a dying winter
Whose old mad drunk cancerous king
Scatters litter like giants' confetti.
Fog's carpet unrolls from Watford to Wimbledon
Oozes into pores of London's brick.
Spring's lazy fingers dab colours
In Royal Park and sooty garden.

Take a cassette, pop it in the Sanyo,
Listen to Fox in crystal form
Shatter the boredom of Sunday heavy Sunday,
Listen to his brisk anecdotes
Spiced with a lifetime's wit.

The heart dances to the silenced voice—
Time *then* dissolves into time *now*.
Time future seems almost bearable,
Hope invades the laughing room

And Fox's words shall have no ending.

LAST POST*

Now the fact seems diamond hard,
This time the Captain's really dead.
Two German doctors signed the death certificate,
Press, radio, T.V. have not disputed it.
The Times has sent Fox off in style—
A favourable obit and two appreciations.
The world's press echoed them.
Yet still an air of mystery surrounds
The Captain's death in Freiburg.

A memorial service has been arranged:
At Margaret's, Westminster, in London's heart.
It's said the PM will be there—
Also a dashing Royal Duke
Will hear the *Last Post* sounded.

Now Fox's friends must patiently collect
Each piece of the mosaic of a life
That still has baffling gaps.
Already the Yale-men are hard at work
Forging a scholar's key for Fox's door.
One day a monolith of Yankee print
Will tell us all—or not a bloody thing.

TWENTIETH-CENTURY CAPTAIN FOX

I was wrong. Absolutely wrong.
Carrington-Smythe was wrong.
All who knew Fox were wrong.
We did not know him well enough.
He was the classic Englishman,
Well-spoken, modest, tolerant,
Who always knew the Test Match score.
His bright intellect dimmed slightly
To match his cronies at the Club.
Yet one or two of us could sense
A distance, a hidden tension.
Why did he read Kafka, Rilke,
Listen to Mozart and Alban Berg,
Try his hand at philosophic comment?
'An English eccentric', said Carrington-Smythe
As he sipped cognac on a Suffolk lawn.
Now the cat has jumped from Hubermann's bag,
His biography a continent of facts,
A mausoleum for the Captain.
Both Fox's parents Jews?
Both victims of the Holocaust?
Young Fox surviving through the *Kindertransport*?
We were dubious, we laughed it off.
That Swiss professor must be daft!
But Hubermann has proved his case
With thirty pages of footnotes,
Documents, eyewitness reports.
Bankers' Zürich has unveiled the truth,
The tragic, the prosaic truth,
The provincial banality of evil.
How wrong we were, how unseeing.
Fox now stands forth as hero, anti-hero,
A self-invented twentieth-century man
Whose business was never my business.

LUNCH AT THE IVY

(2002)

CARTOGRAPHERS

Old men are cartographers.
We map the coloured countries
Our childhood dreamed of.
Down the corridors of years
We see the streets of freedom
Where pirates and cowboys roam;
The tram that clangs to Eden,
The ships heading for exotic ports:
Marseilles, Piraeus, St. Petersburg.
Lands and seas light up
As we lie in the dark,
Hopping from country to country.
Old men before and after sleep
Draw maps, hear distant voices.
River gods and Sirens sing us
To islands, deltas, archipelagos.

BLUE PLAQUES

X, the great composer, was born here.
Y, the Nobel physicist, died in this house.
Z, the famous poet, wrote here in his prime.
They all figure in reference books.
They all have been biographed.
They all got their blue plaques.
Their plaques are stared at by Yanks,
Immaculate Japanese click cameras at them,
Our countrymen simply walk by.
Ah Fame, that goddess they lusted after,
Where are they now, the Great and the Good?
Who reads Sir Walter or Alfred Lord Tennyson?
Who remembers Kelvin or Tom Moore
To whom Lord Byron drank a double health?
Yet, perhaps, a phrase or stanza remains,
Perhaps composer X's opera tune is hummed,
Perhaps ohm or watt or Celsius or Fahrenheit
To someone means men not measurements.
Perhaps blue plaques are not wholly daft.

Damn it, I think I'll settle for one myself.

LONDON, 1936

It's 2000 AD as I peer
Through a wall of glass,
Gaze down a corridor
That runs to 1936.
Who is that lad?
Could it be my young self?
He gets off a train in Paddington,
Walks through Sunday-suited London,
Has his first glimpse of the capital,
Solid, unshakeable London—
Bayswater Road every inch bourgeois,
Marble Arch a hymn to Empire.
At Speakers' Corner he comes across
The talk-as-you-please orators
Flanked by grinning bobbies
With red faces, heavy boots.
Voices headline the air:
FREEDOM FOR INDIA!
END IRISH PARTITION!
ON GUARD FOR SPAIN!
VICTORY TO THE WORKERS!
He wanders on and on and on:
Big Ben, Buck House, the Strand,
Fleet Street, Ludgate Circus.
As he roams the imperial streets
Can I hear him murmur
'Sweet Thames! run softly
Till I end my song'?

FIRST MEETING

I caught her glance across the room,
A face etched on an ancient coin
While on the rug Dolores sprawled
Her head loyal between my knees.
I touched the raven Latin hair
Swam in the dark eye pools.

Patricia blonde, a Nordic queen,
Surveyed the guests with regal air,
Talked of her years in France
In Madame de Forceville's château
Before the Nazi panzers came.

How had I stumbled on such worlds
Aeons from provincial innocence?
Which might I try to enter
Or perhaps be chosen for?
Dark or fair, of ice or fire?

Patricia smiled across the room
When tying on her fur-trimmed hood,
Then vanished into night and light.

Did something in me die?
Was there a hint of birth?

THE STRANGER

The bell shrilled in the winter hall.
'That'll be Patricia', said her friend.
He ran down the stairs from the party
To greet this stranger he'd heard of.

She wore a kind of fur-trimmed hood,
Stood tall on the outside step
Of a Georgian house in Raglan Road,
A daughter of the Anglo-Irishry.

Now, after fifty years or more,
That picture flashes on a screen:
A youth in tweed jacket and corduroys,
The girl in the fur-trimmed hood.

She smiles and he smiles back.
'Yes, I'm Patricia', she says.

VARENGEVILLE

If Patricia were still alive
She'd tease out my memories,
Not that I've quite forgotten
Our holiday in Varengeville.
A Frenchman drove us there
With Gallic panache.
We hurtled through Normandy
As if we were off to rescue
The saintly Joan of Arc
From the English goddams.
I played the glouton,
Later punished by a boil
Back in grey London.
We had a second honeymoon
Our love sky-blue
Yet our joy was tarnished.
'C'est un chien', the driver said
As he dragged the body away.
Patricia and I were upset
As we hurtled on through France,
Poplar after poplar after poplar,
To confort moderne in Varengeville.
It was only a dog after all
Yet its death somehow mattered.

SEVEN CATS

*for John Heath-Stubbs**

The parson's cat is a pious cat
In the church he caught a rat.

The doctor's cat is a healthy cat,
Not too lean, not too fat.

The lawyer's cat is a solemn cat,
Sober as a judge he often sat.

The sportsman's cat's an active cat,
Likes to play with ball and bat.

The scholar's cat is a serious cat,
Who sits and ponders on a mat.

The lady's cat is a pampered cat,
Enjoys his gin and a cosy chat.

The poet's cat is a rhyming cat,
Rat, fat, sat, bat, mat, chat.

ONCE UPON A CHRISTMAS

Once upon a Christmas and all the golden bells
ding-donging Bethlehem and the risefall of voices
and the trills of laughter deep in my heart's well trembling
upwards and soundlessly spilling out
over the rooftops and snow on the Christmas cards
and Father Christmas dizzy with chimney errands
and small 'f' father swilling Guinness like a
nippling baby lost in a rainbow haze of betting
windfalls then wiping moustache on navy serge
sleeve and mother bustling and singing Christians Awake!
salute the morn of mornings the day of Christbirth that was
dark and gloomy just like the
others but oh electric fingers on tinselled parcels
and tense teeth snapping through plump flesh of
goose and throat a-gargling in lemonade with champagne
bubbles at the brim and feeling fit to
burst and afternoon heavy as putty and father
stupefied on the shiny horsehair sofa and evening
of cold ham and tinned pineapple-chunks and mother
reading *A Christmas Carol* oh isn't it luvly she
says no one will ever write like Charles Dickens
again no not if I live till a hundred and Dickens bookcased
and cocoa drunk up the squeaking stairs
and at last alone in the darkness listening to
steel-tipped heels cracking the frosty pavements
and sheepcounting ninety-nine a hundred a hundred and
one two three oh in the darkness Christmas
please never never end while the golden bells
ding-dong to Bethlehem and back again in
candlelight once upon once upon a Christmas deep
as dreamland cosy as a feather bed deep deep deep
once upon a Christmas.

ECSTASY

At school the only word I stumbled over
Was 'ecstasy', by making that second 's' a 'c'.
Mr. Marshall ringed the mistake in red.

Later I came across the word in French.
L'extase, with 's' of course, meant sex and sin.
Mon dieu, the bloody word was feminine.
We schoolboys sniggered over 'vocabulaire':
'Maîtresse', 'putain', 'pissoir'.
The French, it seemed, were far from nice.

Now in *The Times*, no less, I read:
PROOF THAT ECSTASY DAMAGES THE BRAIN.
Damage, it's said, to thought, emotion, memory,
According to the whitecoat boys in Baltimore.

How sad I am to know, long out of school
That spell it as you may, the Puritans
Were right to take the view
That ecstasy (or almost anything you crave,
Like cigarettes or gin or certain kinds of sex)
Is very, very bad for you.

CRASH!

A smiling winter day, sun-sprinkled,
Roads flaunt their dry-bone arms,
The engine croons, the city lights
Shepherd us home to dusk and wine
Yet time and chance must rule.
The driver glances down,
Fumbles the wheel, swerves
Right into a bollard.
Crash! crash! crash!
I lie hours-long on a trolley,
The driver, air-bag saved, sits by me,
Mumbles a litany of guilt.
'Shut up!' I shout, 'Just bloody carelessness!
Blame fate, the gods, but not yourself!'
Days pass, I walk the corridors of pain,
Inhabit depression's dim-lit cell,
Snatch at life on the telephone.
Before I sleep I turn and turn,
Questions flood through my mind:
Will there be daffodils this spring?
Will roses scent the summer air?
Will this? Will that ... ?
I freefall into black dreams.

THE FIXER

Some say there never was a Captain Fox.
Well, then I'll call a witness:
One Derek Stanford, poet, sage,
A citizen of London and the world.
He'll swear on any Bible you can find
That he saw Fox as plain could be
In Brighton town with Lord Olivier,
Actors both and men of action too.
He caught some words of Fox:
'Larry, the PM's in a right old tizz.
I told him I could fix it'.
'Quite so', said Lord Olivier,
'You're just the man, old chap'.
They talked a while, these Thespians,
Then laughed, embraced like Latins,
Parted, their business despatched.
Stanford watched their ego-dance,
Knowing he lived in interesting times.

FOLLOWING DARKNESS

Why burn with rage at close of day*
Or act ungently as we turn to clay?
Fine rhetoric can win the heart
But does not comfort those who must depart.
Better to smile at fate, then coast along,
Hoping to follow darkness into song.

from

SHELLEY PLAIN

(2003)

AT NUMBER 24

Ah, did I once see Eliot plain?
Well, yes, I did in 1949
In London's Russell Square
And if it matters, Number 24.
There the St. Louis eagle spread his wings,
A middle-aged future Nobel man.
He talked of poems for an anthology
(Of which I was co-editor)
That F and F* would shortly publish.
I observed the features of clerical cut
That he himself had noted.
How pleasant to nod to *If* and *Perhaps* and *But*,
To hear the organ tones of that slow voice.
How delightful to meet Ezra's Old Possum
And see that mouth both open and shut.
Ah yes, I once saw T.S. Eliot plain.

LUNCH AT THE IVY

An invitation to lunch—and at the *Ivy!*
I spent ten nail-biting minutes
Before he bounced in, Savile Row smart,
In his early fifties still London's pride.
'What will you drink?' he asked,
'Er, a dry sherry', I replied, assuming nonchalance.
'Not very enterprising—how about vodka?'
He hissed in his crystal accent.
I watched him swoop on an ageing actress:
'How marvellous to see you, dahling.
You were simply wonderful last night'.
He acted out his anecdotes,
An entertainer waiting for the laugh,
Brimful of failsafe wit and charm.
'Come back to the rehearsal with me'.
On the First Night I climbed the stairs
To the Haymarket eyrie at the top.
I shyly knocked and waited.
'Come in, dear boy, come in'.
'You were simply wonderful tonight', I said.
He squeezed my hand until it hurt.
Later I nerved myself to write the book
I'd call *The Art of Noël Coward*.

REMEMBERING ADLESTROP*

*for Shirley Toulson**

I, too, remember Adlestrop
Because one Sunday morning
A friend and I drove there—
Yes, it was late June.
We saw the railway nameplate
That Edward Thomas saw
Through the train window.
No one came and no one left
While we were strolling round.
There were cloudlets in the sky.
We heard no blackbird's song.
In Oxfordshire and Gloucestershire
The birds made not a chirp
Yet they sang for Edward Thomas.

NEIGHBOURS—FOR SEAMUS HEANEY

In your birth-year I bought a Remington,
Shyly tapped out romantic verse,
Runes against the lightless nights,
The warplanes in our northern sky.

By odd conspiracy and chance
Five decades on, we are neighbours,
Each anchored in Yeats's Sandymount,
Both servants of the craft and mystery.

NEW MANUSCRIPT POEMS

(2004)

ALLIUMS

If I had a garden I'd plant
Some great-headed alliums,
Each a soldier one metre high,
Defenders of the floral world
Standing erect under huge heads.
In clumps or on border duty
They flaunt their summer uniform.
But is all this sheer romancing
Since, as I say, I haven't got a garden?

If I had a woman in my life
I'd take her by the hand
And lead her into the garden
That I haven't got and hope
She would admire the alliums.
'They're gorgeous', she'd say
And I'd believe her lying words.
But am I just a daft romantic
Since there's neither woman nor garden?

WAITING

*i.m. Andrew Boyd and Stan Smith**

Where have they gone, my friends?
Have they crossed the river,
Each tagged by a sell-by date?
What they'll find on the other side
We can only dream of, guess at.
Dazzling flora in a time-free Eden
Or an acreage of darkness?
Ah, where are those friends of yesterday
Whose chairs and desks are untenanted,
Whose photos crowd my albums?
In my address book I add two crosses
For friends gone over the water.
I wait by the phone hopefully,
Listening for voices from outer space.
Lost friends, I am waiting, waiting.

A REPLY TO MEG*

Meg writes from London—
'You are not English
You are not Irish
You're nearly Scottish
But not even that'.
Meg's Lakeland English
Anglo-Saxon, Norman, Dane.
She asks where I belong.
My ancestors are dubbed
The Ulster Scots,
Settlers yet unsettled
In an alien land
But loyal to their tribe
Their label 'British'.
As for myself—
Nations be damned
A plague on tribes
Passports, border guards,
Slogans on the wall.
I'm only myself.
Trust no nation's will
Outgrow your tribe.
Listen to your heartbeat
Sing your own song
As best you can.

THE MEANING OF LIFE

In the staffroom McCarthy snoozes,
Brown flicks through *The Guardian*,
Bayley stares out at a tree,
Grant prepares his next lesson
On the use of the Future Perfect
('By this time tomorrow I shall have ...')
The telephone rings, Trudgett answers
For he's the lecturer-in-charge.
'Too many tutors already', he snarls.
In the corridor women are talking,
Shrill voices rise in an earnest curve.
'What are those hens clucking about?'
Trudgett asks Grant, who looks startled.
'It's to do with the meaning of life'.
'The meaning of life?' gasps Trudgett.
'I'll tell you the meaning of life'.
Grant coughs into the silence.
'The meaning is that there's no meaning'.
The door swings open, the women enter.
The bell has started to ring.
'Time to get going', says Trudgett.
Out we go, aware of the meaning of time.

THANATOS

The ancients called him Thanatos.
Is he a Fury or a Kindly One?
Some say he's soft as gossamer,
Others that he's leather tough
But all agree he's unpredictable.
Where will he go or send a minion?
Nobody has ever seen this man
Or the HQ where he runs his business,
Speeding agents on secret missions.
Is he tall or short, Caucasian or black?
How does he dress, is he polyglot?
Neither dons nor reference books can tell.
Yet Thanatos is a man of mystery and power.
He's been in touch with friends of mine:
Leslie and Joan, Andrew, Peggy, Stan,
Carrington-Smythe and Captain Fox.
Nobody escapes the eye of Thanatos.
One day he'll visit you—and me.

THE RIVER*

A river of silver wanders
Through green pastureland,
Coasts gently to the ocean.
The glassy water ambles
On its journey to the sea.
Unstoppable the river runs
On its quiet mission
Until the goal is reached
And son rejoins his mother.

END NOTES

The Bird, line 32: The deceased farmer is imagined. The bird is the banshee.

Cycling to Dublin, dedication: Leslie Gillespie was a boyhood friend of Greacen's. Later, in London, he wrote a number of novels. One of the novels, *The Man from Madura* (London: 1952), was published.

Ulster, line 16: describing the Harland and Wollf shipyard, builders of the Titanic.

The Far Country, line 16: The poem has some echoes of Yeats's Byzantium poems.

Poem to K.D., line 1: Kay Dick was a London friend of R.G.'s and a novelist.

Lines for Friends, line 19: 'whin' is an Ulster word for 'furze' or 'gorse'.

Michael Walked in the Wood, line 28: Michael is an imagined character.

Captain Fox, line 5: 'Gauloise' is a strong French cigarette. Its strength is supposed to connote masculinity; its gold tip quality. Line 8: 'pre-Ayer' refers to A. J. Ayer, who, with Bertrand Russell, was a Logical Positivist or Empiricist in England during the 1940s and '50s. His view was that ethical values relate only to the person holding them.

Captain Fox on J. Edgar Hoover, line 17: These are real or imagined enemies of J. Edgar Hoover. They fit into three categories: petty gangsters (Ma and Pa Barker, John Dillinger, 'Pretty Boy' Floyd, 'Machine Gun' Kelly, and 'Baby Face' Nelson); spies (Frederick Duquesne, Alvin Karpis, Julius and Ethel Rosenberg, Harry Gold, Colonel Abel); and organised crime (Joe Valachi). Many of these made Hoover's 'public enemy #1' list).

The Traveller, line 2: Norton Fitzwarren and Shepton Mallet are small villages in Somerset. Sheepwash and Black Torrington are small villages in Devon.

Curse, line 9: Scots phrase meaning a churchyard that is comfortable or blessed. Line 13, John Logie Baird, who lived in 1888-1946, was a television pioneer and credited by some as its inventor.

A Poet Dying, dedication: Clifford Dyment, fellow poet and friend who wrote the introduction for the first version of the Greacen memoir, *Even Without Irene* (Dolmen, 1969).

Auden, line 10: 'skald' is from old Norse, meaning 'poet'.

Old Zechariah, title: Old Zechariah was the father of John the Baptist (see *Luke* 1:5, 67; 3:2).

A Man Called Simeon, title: Simeon recognised the divinity and suspected the future martyrdom of Jesus (Luke 2:25-35).

The Photographer, line 7: 'Wodge' is Scottish for thick lump or chunk.

Uncle George, line 3: 'sheugh' is Scottish for 'ditch'.

Uncle Jack, line 21: moquette is a French carpet with thick, red nap; line 22: Axminster carpets are English carpets with a cut pile, often hand-woven.

Instead of Flowers, line 6: a 'tawse' is a leather lash or whip with several tails.

Church and Covenant, line 1: the British use of 'kitschy' means pretentious and therefore shallow. The American usage of the word is slightly different, more as 'tasteless and ostentatious'. Greacen, of course, meant the British usage.

Comrade Ted, dedication: Thomas McCarthy is an Irish poet, born in County Waterford in 1954.

Kinsky, line 28: Kinsky is an imagined character.

At the Garrick Club, line 5: referring to Mrs. Patrick Campbell, a turn-of-the-twentieth-century actress; line 11: 'souk' is an Arabic term for an open-air marketplace in North Africa.

The Only Emperor, line 30: in Stevens's poem, the only emperor is death.

Kavanagh in Ballsbridge, title: Greacen's account of meeting Patrick Kavanagh in Dublin.

Opening the Door, dedication: Beatrice Behan was Brendan Behan's widow and Greacen's Anglesea Road landlady.

Queen of the Bucket Shop, dedication: Jack Midgley, a Belfast contemporary and friend.

The Call, dedication: 'The Call' was composed in Rock Hill, South Carolina, USA. It evokes Greacen's life and replies to Stephen Spender's 'What I Expected', a part of which was the epigraph in R.G.'s *Collected Poems 1944-1994*.

At Brendan Behan's Desk, line 15: 'Cuig' in Irish means 'five'; here it also is to be recognised as a street address.

Operation Jubilee, line 1: 'French citizens! This is a raid and not the invasion'; line 7, 'Gamekeepers. Bar entrance under pain of prosecution'.

Last Post, title: Given its subject matter, 'Last Post' appropriately appeared in *Captain Fox: A Life*, though it was first published as part of *Young Mr. Gibbon* (1979).

Seven Cats, dedication: John Heath-Stubbs, an English poet and friend of Greacen's.

Following Darkness, line 1: The poem answers Dylan Thomas's 'Do Not Go Gentle Into That Good Night'.

At Number 24, line 9: 'F and F' is Faber and Faber, for whom Eliot served as director.

Remembering Adlestrop, title: a town in Oxfordshire; dedication: Shirley Toulson, Oxford friend and specialist in folklore. *Lunch at the Ivy* (2002) is dedicated to her.

Waiting, dedication: Andrew Boyd, a Scottish/English writer, was R.G.'s colleague at the United Nations Association in London. Stan Smith was a London librarian.

A Reply to Meg, title: Meg Watkins is a London friend of Robert Greacen's.

The River, title: 'Thanatos' (death) and 'The River' appropriately end the volume of *Selected & New Poems*. As will be clear to the reader, these final six poems are a gathering of themes from Greacen's life. As such, they also echo ideas in poems throughout his career.

DATE			